T0348387

Timothy Keller

Galatians

Gospel Matters

7-Session Bible Study

Galatians For You

These studies are adapted from *Galatians For You*. If you are reading *Galatians For You* alongside this Good Book Guide, here is how the studies in this booklet link to the chapters of *Galatians For You*:

Study One > Ch 1

Study Two > Ch 2-3

Study Three > Ch 4

Study Four > Ch 5-6

Study Five > Ch 7-9

Study Six > Ch 10-11

Study Seven > Ch 12-13

Find out more about *Galatians For You* at:
www.thegoodbook.com/for-you

Galatians: Gospel Matters

A Good Book Guide

© Timothy Keller/The Good Book Company, 2013.

This edition printed 2025.

Published by The Good Book Company

thegoodbook.com | thegoodbook.co.uk

thegoodbook.com.au | thegoodbook.co.nz | thegoodbook.co.in

Unless indicated, all Scripture references are taken from the Holy Bible, New International Version. Copyright © 2011 Biblica. Used by permission.

All rights reserved. Except as may be permitted by the Copyright Act, no part of this publication may be reproduced in any form or by any means without prior permission from the publisher.

Timothy Keller has asserted his right under the Copyright, Designs and Patents Act 1988 to be identified as author of this work.

A CIP catalogue record for this book is available from the British Library.

Design by André Parker and Drew McCall

ISBN: 9781802541670 | JOB-008033 | Printed in India

Contents

 # Introduction

One of the Bible writers described God's word as "a lamp for my feet, a light on my path" (Psalm 119:105, NIV). God gave us the Bible to tell us about who he is and what he wants for us. He speaks through it by his Spirit and lights our way through life.

That means that we need to look carefully at the Bible and uncover its meaning—but we also need to apply what we've discovered to our lives.

Good Book Guides are designed to help you do just that. The sessions in this book are interactive and easy to lead. They're perfect for use in groups or for personal study.

Let's take a look at what is included in each session.

Talkabout: Every session starts with an ice-breaker question, designed to get people talking around a subject that links to the Bible study.

Investigate: These questions help you explore what the passage is about.

Apply: These questions are designed to get you thinking practically: what does this Bible teaching mean for you and your church?

Explore More: These optional sections help you to go deeper or to explore another part of the Bible which connects with the main passage.

Getting Personal: These sections are a chance for personal reflection. Some groups may feel comfortable discussing these, but you may prefer to look at them quietly as individuals instead—or leave them out.

Pray: Here, you're invited to pray in the light of the truths and challenges you've seen in the study.

Each session is also designed to be easily split into two! Watch out for the **Apply** section that comes halfway through, and stop there if you haven't got time to do the whole thing in one go.

In the back of the book, you'll find a **Leader's Guide**, which provides helpful notes on every question, along with everything else that group leaders need in order to facilitate a great session and help the group uncover the riches of God's light-giving word.

Why Study Galatians?

Which gospel are you relying on?

In Galatia in AD 50, the church faced a choice between two "gospels"— two ways of living, of thinking, of viewing how to be right with God.

On the one side were the teachers who told these young Christians that their performance mattered. Of course they needed to trust Christ and his death; and then, if they wanted truly to be acceptable to God, they needed to get circumcised and get on with keeping God's laws. Their efforts were what counted.

On the other side was Paul, the church-planting missionary who had founded the Galatian church a few years before. He said they were "foolish" and "bewitched" (3:1). He claimed the gospel they were turning to was actually "no gospel at all" (1:7).

And he told them that the only performance that mattered was Christ's: his life, death, and resurrection. Faith in him, Paul argued, was all that anyone needed to be truly acceptable to God. Their efforts counted for nothing— and relying on them would bring them under God's "curse" (3:10). Which "gospel" they followed mattered.

The choice between the gospel of Christ-alone and the false gospel of Christ-plus is still one which Christians face today. Christ-plus may not look the same in our cultures as it did in Galatia. But it's still an attractive message, a flattering view, and a subtle reversal of the true gospel... and so it's still deadly.

As Paul wrote to the Galatian church, he knew that to lose your grip on the true gospel is to desert and lose Christ himself, and to lose the salvation and blessing and freedom he gives. The gospel matters. Paul knew that everything was at stake.

It still is. In these seven studies taking you through the book of Galatians, Paul will present us with a gospel that is wonderful, liberating, and true. He'll show us that our problems in the Christian life come when we lose or forget or fail to live by this gospel.

And he will ask us repeatedly: which gospel are you relying on?

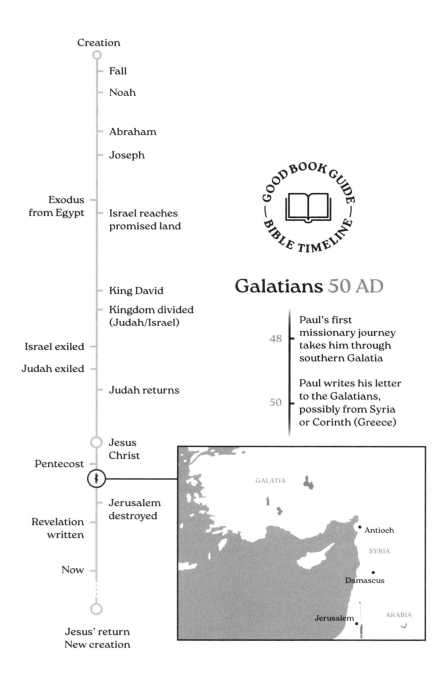

Creation

Fall

Noah

Abraham

Joseph

Exodus from Egypt

Israel reaches promised land

King David

Kingdom divided (Judah/Israel)

Israel exiled

Judah exiled

Judah returns

Jesus Christ

Pentecost

Jerusalem destroyed

Revelation written

Now

Jesus' return
New creation

GOOD BOOK GUIDE · BIBLE TIMELINE

Galatians 50 AD

48 — Paul's first missionary journey takes him through southern Galatia

50 — Paul writes his letter to the Galatians, possibly from Syria or Corinth (Greece)

GALATIA

Antioch

SYRIA

Damascus

Jerusalem

ARABIA

1

Gospel Reversed

Galatians 1:1-9

Talkabout

1. What makes you surprised or disappointed?

Investigate

📖 **Read Galatians 1:1-9**

DICTIONARY

Grace (v 3): unmerited favor.   **Pervert** (v 7): reverse, twist.
Gospel (v 6): announcement (often
of good news).

2. As Paul begins this letter, what does his mood seem to be?

- What reasons do these verses give for his frame of mind?

3. How does Paul describe himself in verse 1? What does verse 1 tell us about what he means by this word?

Explore More | OPTIONAL

📖 **Read Romans 1:8-10; 1 Corinthians 1:4-7; Ephesians 1:15-17; Philippians 1:3-8; Colossians 1:3-6**

- What do all these have in common that the beginning of Galatians is lacking?
- How do you think Paul would have wanted the Galatian Christians to respond to this omission?
- How does this change how we read the letter to the Galatians?

---

4. Galatians 1:1-5 contains the core of Paul's "gospel," or announcement. So from these verses, what is "the gospel"?

- Why does this gospel bring people "grace and peace … from God" (v 3), do you think?

• Who gets the glory and praise for the gospel? Why is this fair?

Apply

5. Verse 5 is the motivation for everything Paul does. How is this a challenge to us?

Getting Personal | OPTIONAL

If someone asked you what the gospel is, what would you say? Why not write down your explanation of the gospel sometime today, and use verses 1-5 to help you shape and sharpen it.

Who will you ask God to give you an opportunity to share the gospel with this week?

Investigate

We've seen that Paul is "astonished" that the Galatian church is "turning to a different gospel" (v 6).

6. Read Galatians 3:1-5. How do some teachers in Galatia seem to have been changing the gospel message?

7. What does Paul say about any change to the gospel message (1:6-7)?

- Why is this the case, do you think?

8. What is Paul's attitude to those who "pervert" the gospel (v 8-9)?

- Think about what we've seen the real gospel is; gives us; and results in for God. Do you think Paul's language here is justified? Why / why not?

9. When did the Galatians hear the real "gospel of Christ" (v 8)? How does verse 1 give us confidence that this gospel is the true gospel?

Apply

10. How do people today add to the gospel message?

11. Why do we sometimes not react to false gospels in the same way as Paul did?

Getting Personal | OPTIONAL

The gospel message cannot be changed without being lost. It's like a vacuum—as soon as you let air into a vacuum, it is no vacuum at all.

In what ways are you tempted to add to the gospel of Jesus Christ crucified and risen, our rescuer and ruler?

How much do you care when you hear someone changing the gospel message? Is your attitude like Paul's? Why / why not?

12. Why is the real gospel wonderful?!

Pray

Thank God for...

- *appointing apostles to preach and defend the gospel.*
- *Paul's commitment to and passion for gospel truth.*
- *the gospel. Thank God for rescuing his people from their sins through the death of his Son, and raising him from the dead to prove forgiveness is available.*

Ask God...

- *to deepen your love and passion for the gospel.*
- *to help you to recognize false, reversed gospels; and to have the wisdom to know how to respond.*
- *for opportunities to share the true gospel with others this week.*

2

Gospel-Given Unity

Galatians 1:10 - 2:10

The Story So Far...

Paul is astonished that the Galatian churches are reversing the true gospel, which brings grace and peace for us, and glory to God.

Talkabout

1. Is church unity important, and why? Is church unity ever a bad thing?

Investigate

📖 **Read Galatians 1:10-24**

DICTIONARY

Revelation (v 12): message from God.
Zealous (v 14): passionate about.
Gentiles (v 16): non-Jews.
Get acquainted (v 18): get to know.

Cephas (Peter) and **James** (v 18-19): two leaders of the Jerusalem church.
Judea (v 22): the area around Jerusalem.

In this section (and all the way to 2:21), Paul gives us a (very short!) autobiography.

2. What does he tell us about…
   • his life before becoming a Christian?

   • how he became a Christian?

   • what he did after becoming a Christian?

3. Think about what kind of person Paul had been. What is amazing, and wonderful, about verses 15-16a?

Getting Personal | OPTIONAL

Solitary time with God, as Paul had in Arabia, is crucial in developing our relationship with God. But we live in a time that puts too much emphasis on activity and accomplishment.

Are you spending time with God, reading his word and praying?

Do you take time in your day to meditate on your identity as his child? Do you take time at the end of your day to reflect on it, thanking him for his grace and admitting your failings?

We've seen that "some people" (v 7) were suggesting to the Galatians that they shouldn't trust Paul's teaching.

4. What kinds of claims about himself does Paul seem to be answering here in these verses?

5. What result of a gospel-changed life does verse 10 show us?

Apply

6. When do we find it hard to be a God-pleaser rather than a man-pleaser? Why?

• How will remembering the gospel that saved Paul, and saved us, free us from being driven by man's approval?

Investigate

📖 **Read Galatians 2:1-10**

DICTIONARY

Circumcised (v 3): in the Old Testament, God told the men among his people to be circumcised to show they were trusting and obeying him.
Infiltrated (v 4): sneaked in unnoticed.

Reputed to be pillars (v 9): said to be important.
Fellowship (v 9): unity and friendship.

When Paul went "to Jerusalem" (v 1), it wasn't because he was afraid his message was wrong. He was an apostle, receiving "revelation" (v 2) from God—he didn't need to check it with anyone else! But he was afraid he "had run my race in vain" (v 2).

As we saw in session 1, "false brothers" (v 4) were teaching that faith in Christ was not enough, saying, *You are saved by both faith in Jesus and obedience to Jewish law—laws such as needing to be circumcised.* If the church leaders in Jerusalem agreed with them, the church would split into Gentile and Jewish, into "faith alone" and "faith plus works."

7. Why was the Jerusalem leaders' decision about Titus (v 3) so significant?

- If they had agreed with the "false brothers" and made the opposite decision, how would "the truth of the gospel" have been lost?

8. What did the apostles in Jerusalem recognize about Paul (v 6-9)?

9. How does this episode show the importance of pursuing unity within the church?

- How does it show us the limits of pursuing unity? (Verses 4-5 will help.)

Explore More | OPTIONAL

Both Paul and the Jerusalem leaders made the poor a priority (v 10).

📖 **Read Leviticus 23:22 and Deuteronomy 15:7-8**

- How were God's people in the land of Israel to treat the poor among them?

📖 **Read 1 John 3:16-17 and 2 Corinthians 8:8-15**

- How are God's people today to treat the poor among us?
- What example does 2 Corinthians give us?

📖 **Read Matthew 5:43-48 and 25:31-46**

- What does caring for the poor, and not caring for the poor, show about us?
- Why is it right that the apostles made it a priority to agree to "remember the poor" (Galatians 2:10)? How does this challenge you individually, and as a local church?

Apply

10. In what ways does the gospel give people freedom that "earn your salvation" religions don't?

11. This passage shows us several differences that knowing and loving the true gospel makes. What would these things look like in your life and church community today?
    - 1:10

    - 1:24

- 2:9-10

Getting Personal | OPTIONAL

Though spending solitary time with God is a fundamental part of the Christian life, the Christian life is not fundamentally a solitary one.

Church commitment and church unity matter.

How deeply rooted are you in church life? What are you doing to maintain, and show, unity with fellow believers?

When might you be in danger of picking and choosing what you feel you need from church life, rather than serving others throughout church life?

Pray

Thank God for...

- *how he saved each one of you. (Share a little of your stories before praying if you like.)*
- *for the unity you have with other Christians from every background and culture.*

Ask God...

- *to help you remember you have his approval, and don't need anyone else's.*
- *to make you truly committed to pleasing him and serving his people.*

3

Gospel: The A-Z

Galatians 2:11-21

The Story So Far...

Paul is astonished that the Galatian churches are reversing the true gospel, which brings grace and peace for us, and glory to God.

God worked in Paul before saving him, and equipped him to preach the gospel. His trip to Jerusalem proved that the apostolic gospel is all about faith in Christ.

Talkabout

1. Who needs the gospel, and what difference does it make to them?

Investigate

📖 **Read Galatians 2:11-21**

DICTIONARY

Circumcision group (v 12): teachers who said you needed to be circumcised as well as trust in Jesus in order to be acceptable to God.
Hypocrisy (v 13): believing or saying one thing, and then doing the opposite.

Law (v 16): God's commands about how to live in relationship with him, found in the Old Testament.
Justified (v 16-17): made, or declared, completely innocent.
Righteousness (v 21): here, Paul means the status of being in a right relationship with God.

2. Peter (Cephas) was one of Jesus' closest friends, who had seen him teach, heal, live, die, and rise. What is surprising about verse 11?

- What was Peter doing that caused Paul to act like this (v 12-15)?

3. How did Paul view Peter's and Barnabas' actions (v 14a)?

- What is significant about this insight, do you think?

Explore More | OPTIONAL

📖 Read Acts 11:1-18

- Why did Peter originally begin eating with Gentiles?
- What was so significant about this vision (v 18)?
- How does this make his actions in Galatians 2:12 even worse?

Apply

4. What are the ways in which we can insist other Christians act as we do (or even hold them to a higher standard than we hold ourselves)?

- What are the reasons why we find ourselves doing this? (Verse 12 gives us one motivation.)

Getting Personal | OPTIONAL

Do you need to change your attitude towards, or treatment of, other people in light of your answers to question 4? How will you do this?

Investigate

5. In verses 15-16, what does Paul remind Peter about…
   - following God's commands?

   - having faith in Jesus?

   - How do these verses shed light on the meaning of the word "justification"?

6. What is the objection Paul raises to "justification by faith" in verse 17? Why is it a fair point to make?

Verses 18-21 are Paul's answer to this question. And verse 18 is difficult! It probably means, *If someone keeps on with the same lifestyle after supposedly receiving Christ, it proves they really did not grasp the gospel, but were only looking for an excuse to disobey God.*

But verses 19-21 bear most of Paul's argument, and are very powerful, so we're going to focus on those for the rest of the study.

It was "through the law" (v 19)—that is, as he tried to obey it, and realized he would never manage it—that Paul understood that the law could not be his savior.

7. Paul suggests in verse 19 that when he was trying to save himself by obeying the law, he was not able to "live for God." Why is this, do you think?

- Now Paul has "died to the law" as the way to save himself, because he knows that Christ and not his own obedience is what saves him. Why does this mean he is now able to truly "live for God"?

8. What does verse 20a tell us has happened to a Christian's old, sinful self? Who does God see when he looks at a Christian?

- What difference does this make to the way a Christian lives (v 20)?

9. Try to put verse 21 into your own words.

Apply

10. From these verses, what is "the truth of the gospel"?

• Who needs it? (Remember verses 11-14.)

• What difference does it make for our lives?

11. In what areas of life do you find it most difficult to live "in line with the truth of the gospel"?

Paul helped Peter by pointing him to the gospel of justification by faith. He didn't just tell him he was getting it wrong!

12. How might you use the gospel to respond to a Christian saying the following things?

- "Jesus saved me, and now I am living his way to continue to earn his forgiveness."

- "I get angry when someone cuts me off when I'm driving. It's just so rude."

- "Teenagers who become Christians must learn to like long sermons."

Getting Personal | OPTIONAL

How do you view the gospel—as your ticket to future heaven, or a manifesto for all of life today?

It is our job to bring everything in our lives—our thinking, feelings, and behavior—"in line" with the gospel.

Is this something you are consciously doing? Each morning, do you look forward to your day and consider how the gospel will impact what you do and how you do it?

Pray

Thank God that faith in Christ is all you need to be justified with him.

Ask God to help you see how to live out the gospel in every area of your life; and to show you any ways in which you are expecting other Christians to add works to their faith.

4

The Gospel and the Law

Galatians 3:1-25

The Story So Far...

Paul is astonished that the Galatian churches are reversing the true gospel, which brings grace and peace for us, and glory to God.

God worked in Paul before saving him, and equipped him to preach the gospel. His trip to Jerusalem proved that the apostolic gospel is all about faith in Christ.

When Peter didn't live all his life in line with the gospel of justification by faith, Paul challenged him to let the gospel shape his attitudes and actions.

Talkabout

1. What is the point of God's law?

Investigate

📖 **Read Galatians 3:1-5**

DICTIONARY

Portrayed (v 1): explained, shown to be.

---

2. What are the answers to Paul's questions in verses 1-5?

- What point is he making to the Galatians?

Apply

3. What do these verses tell us about how we grow as Christians?

Investigate

📖 **Read Galatians 3:6-14**

DICTIONARY

Blessed (v 8): in this context, a life of enjoying knowing God and living under his rule in his world.

Book of the Law (v 10): the first five books of the Bible.
Redeemed (v 13-14): bought back.

---

4. How did Abraham (here, Abram) become right with God (v 6)?

- How was this a model for the Galatians—people who were non-Jewish, living 1,500 years after Abraham?

Explore More | OPTIONAL

📖 **Read Genesis 15:1-21**

- What does Abraham (called Abram here) believe God will do, despite the fact he's nearly 100 years old (v 4-6)?

He's trusting God to fulfill his promises (see 12:1-3). It's this kind of faith that God responds to by making people righteous (15:6).

- What does Abraham have to do (v 9-11)?

Fire is a sign of God's presence. And the passing through animal pieces was an ancient way of sealing a binding agreement—a covenant.

Usually, both parties would pass between the animal pieces, as a way of saying that they would die if the covenant was broken by them.

- What passes through this alleyway (v 17)? Who doesn't (v 12)?!
- What is God showing about who will keep this covenant? Why is that good news for imperfect Abraham?

In Galatians 3:12, Paul says, "The man who does these things will live by them." To "live by" something means to rely on it for our happiness and fulfilment. It's what gives us meaning, confidence, and definition.

5. What does living by, or relying on, observing the law lead to?

- Why is this, do you think?

6. If verse 10 is true, how can God credit us as righteous without being unjust (v 13)?

• What does trusting in Christ's death give us (v 14)? Why is this exciting?

Getting Personal | OPTIONAL

Have you appreciated that, if you trust in Christ, you are living a life of blessing, and are not under any divine or emotional curse?

What causes you to become anxious, or envious, or despairing? How will remembering you are redeemed and blessed by God through his Son, and filled with his Spirit, help direct your emotions at those points?

📖 Read Galatians 3:15-25

DICTIONARY

Covenant (v 15): a binding agreement, like a marriage or will.
Seed (v 16): a future member of your family tree.
Transgressions (v 19): sins.
Mediator (v 19-20): someone who takes two people (or groups) who are enemies, and does what is necessary to make them friends.
Impart (v 21): give.
Guardianship or **supervision** (NIV84) (v 25): the word literally means "tutelage," i.e. the care of a teacher.

Moses was given the law by God 430 years after God's promises of salvation to Abraham. So isn't the law an improvement on, or replacement for, the promises? If it is, we need to obey the law to be saved!

7. How does Paul answer this objection (v 15-18)?

8. What doesn't the law achieve (v 21)?

- What does the law achieve (v 22-23)?

- So, what is the point of the law (v 24-25)?!

9. "We are no longer under the supervision of the law" (NIV84). Does this mean Christians shouldn't be concerned about obeying the law, do you think? Why / why not? (Hint: 2:19-20 might help you here.)

Apply

10. Why do people need to know that God is a God who has laws, before they can understand why Jesus' death is good news?

11. How might a professing Christian believer end up coming under the curse of law-observance without realizing it?

• What would you say to someone who has done this?

Getting Personal | OPTIONAL

How has this passage motivated you...
- to love Jesus?
- to obey the law?
- to tell others the gospel?

Pray

"Christ redeemed us from the curse of the law by becoming a curse for us ... He redeemed us in order that the blessing given to Abraham might come to the Gentiles through Christ Jesus." (3:13-14)

Spend some time as a group thanking God for all he has taken from you and given to you in the Lord Jesus.

5

Gospel Adoption

Galatians 3:26 – 4:31

The Story So Far...

God worked in Paul before saving him, and equipped him to preach the gospel. His trip to Jerusalem proved that the apostolic gospel is all about faith in Christ.

When Peter didn't live all his life in line with the gospel of justification by faith, Paul challenged him to let the gospel shape his attitudes and actions.

Paul urged the Galatians to keep trusting Jesus, who has done what the law cannot. He has taken our divine and emotional curse, giving us God's blessing.

Talkabout

1. If you asked 100 people what the difference is between Christianity and other religions, what answers do you think you would get?

- What would you say is the difference (if any)?

Investigate

📖 **Read Galatians 3:26 – 4:7**

DICTIONARY

Children (3:26): the original word here means "sons," i.e. legal heirs.
Gentile (v 28): non-Jew.
Elemental spiritual forces or **basic principles** (NIV84) (4:3): Paul means a belief system that says we must save ourselves, by worshiping fake gods or by trying to keep religious rules.
Abba (v 6): "Dad" or "Papa."

---

2. Who is a child (or son—see NIV84) of God, and why (3:26-27)?

3. Why is it wonderful to be a son of God?
   - 3:29

   - 4:1-5, 7

   - 4:6

4. What is the connection between the work of the Son and the Spirit (v 4-7)?

Apply

5. When we don't feel joyful as Christians, or loved by God, what do we need to do?

Getting Personal | OPTIONAL

The astonishing bottom line of sonship is that God now treats us as though we have done everything that Jesus has done. We can approach God as if we were as faithful, beautiful and heroic as Jesus himself. We are heirs with him. To God, we look like him.

- How does this make you feel?
- How will you make sure you meditate on the reality and privilege of sonship each day of the rest of your life?

Investigate

📖 **Read Galatians 4:8-20**

DICTIONARY

Observing (v 10): keeping.
Testify (v 15): give evidence.

Perplexed (v 20): really puzzled.

The Galatians had become Christians out of a pagan, idolatrous background. Now they are in danger of turning to a Judaistic law-keeping religion.

6. But what does Paul say they're turning to in verses 8-10?

- What is the implication of what Paul's saying here?

Explore More | OPTIONAL

- How does Paul describe his relationship with these Galatians?
  - v 13-14
  - v 15-16
- How does his ministry differ from that of the false teachers…
  - in its goal?
  - in its means?
- What does this teach us about true, faithful gospel ministry?

📖 Read Galatians 4:21-31

DICTIONARY

Taken figuratively (v 24): used as an image to explain something.
Covenants (v 24): here, Paul means "ways of relating to God".
Mount Sinai (v 24): the place where God gave his people his law, as they traveled to the promised land.

Hagar (v 24, 25): Abraham's servant and the mother of his son Ishmael—the "slave woman" of verse 22.
Isaac (v 28): the son of Sarah, Abraham's wife—who is the "free woman" of verse 22.

Paul has taught the Galatian Christians that they were fully children of Abraham the moment they believed in Christ. The false teachers had taught them that they had to submit to all the Old Testament laws, including circumcision, to really be children of Abraham.

So now Paul makes his point in one final, dramatic way, by comparing Abraham's two sons: Ishmael and Isaac (v 22).

7. Read Genesis 16:1-4; 18:10-14; 21:1-10. What are the differences between the births of these two sons?

• How much faith did Abraham need to have a son with Hagar? How much did he need to have a son with Sarah?

8. What does Paul say each mother represents (Galatians 4:24-26)? Why?

• The residents of Jerusalem would have thought of Sarah as their mother, and Hagar as the mother of unrighteous Gentiles. Why does this give extra force to what Paul says here?

9. What is Paul saying the Galatians should expect (v 28-29)?

Apply

10. Why do both non-religious and religious people need the gospel?

- Why do religious people persecute gospel people (v 29), do you think?

Getting Personal | OPTIONAL

Do you believe that you can never be so good, or moral, that you won't need the gospel of Christ crucified anymore?

Do you believe that no one is too bad, or too religious, to be able to be saved by the gospel?

How do your answers to those two questions affect how you feel about yourself and about others?

Pray

Thank God for…

Confess to God…

Ask God…

6

Gospel Freedom, Gospel Fruit

Galatians 5:1-25

The Story So Far...

When Peter didn't live all his life in line with the gospel of justification by faith, Paul challenged him to let the gospel shape his attitudes and actions.

Paul urged the Galatians to keep trusting Christ, who has done what the law cannot. He has taken our divine and emotional curse, giving us God's blessing.

Believers in Jesus are clothed with Jesus, and are sons of God. Christians are free to enjoy having God's Spirit, and look forward to their inheritance.

Talkabout

1. Why does a child obey his or her parents?

Investigate

📖 **Read Galatians 5:1-15**

Yoke (v 1): put over the back of an ox to control it.
Alienated from (v 4): isolated from, nothing to do with.

Emasculate (v 12): literally, castrate!
Indulge (v 13): do whatever someone wants.

2. What has Christ done (v 1)?

- What should be our response to this?

3. What are the expressions of real saving faith—and what aren't (v 5-6)?

Paul has warned these Christians not to give up their freedom (v 1) by returning to the slavery of trying to earn their salvation. But he also tells them not to abuse their freedom.

4. What should they use their gospel freedom to do (v 13-14)?

- How does the gospel free us truly to love God and others, do you think?

- How does it motivate us to love God and others, do you think?

Apply

5. How might we obey God, but for wrong or inadequate reasons?

Getting Personal | OPTIONAL

Look at your answers to question 5. When might you obey God for these reasons?

You don't have to obey God at all—but the gospel means we want to! How will you use the gospel to change your motive for obedience?

Explore More | OPTIONAL

In verse 7, Paul compares the Christian life to a race. The Galatian believers had started well, but had been pushed off course.

📖 **Read Philippians 3:12-14; Hebrews 12:1-3**

- What do these passages tell us about how to keep running the Christian race?
- How do they motivate us to keep running?

Investigate

📖 **Read Galatians 5:16-25**

DICTIONARY

Gratify (v 16): do whatever someone wants.
Contrary (v 17): opposite.
Under law (v 18): relying on keeping God's law to be saved.
Debauchery (v 19): uncontrolled sexuality.

Discord (v 20): picking fights.
Dissensions (v 20): creating and continuing arguments.
Factions (v 20): promoting divisions between groups.

6. What is going on inside every Christian (v 16-17)?

• What is encouraging about this truth? What is challenging?

Literally, "desires" (v 16-17) means "over-desires"—when we feel we must have something. It is an all-controlling drive or longing for something—treating a good thing as though it is a god thing.

7. What does this tell us about how our sinful nature works?

8. Look at the "acts of the sinful nature" in verses 19-21. Pick out two or three, and think about how they are consequences of "over-desire."

Getting Personal | OPTIONAL

Which "acts" in verses 19-21 do you struggle with?

Don't simply try to change your behavior or your feelings. Ask yourself: Why I am I gratifying my sinful nature in this way? How am I looking to get myself security or satisfaction or significance, rather than allowing Jesus to give it to me?

Remember that through faith you are a son of God (3:26). How will that take away your motivation to sin?

9. Pick a couple of the aspects of the fruit of the Spirit from verses 22-23. How are these things products of believing the gospel? How are they aspects of serving others in love?

10. What is our part in producing these qualities? What is the Spirit's part (v 18, 22, 25)?

Getting Personal | OPTIONAL

Which of the segments of this fruit do you particularly need to ask God to grow in you through his Spirit?

How will dwelling on the truths of the gospel help produce this fruit in you?

Apply

11. Which of the acts of the sinful nature are most common, and most acceptable, in your culture?

12. Which aspects of the fruit of the Spirit are least noticed and celebrated within your church?

- What would these look like in action?

Pray

Thank God for the freedom you have as his son to serve him and love others. Thank him for putting his Spirit in you. Thank him for the fruit that you can see him growing in the members of your group.

Confess to God (out loud or silently) the ways in which you gratify your sinful nature instead of keeping in step with the Spirit; and thank him that you are saved by grace, not by works.

Ask God to work through his Spirit to grow gospel fruit in you. Talk to him about any people you know, individually or as a group, who need to be served in love, and ask him for help to do that, freely and joyfully.

7

The Gospel Is Enough

Galatians 5:26 - 6:18

The Story So Far...

Paul urged the Galatians to keep trusting Christ, who has done what the law cannot. He has taken our divine and emotional curse, giving us God's blessing.

Believers in Jesus are clothed with Jesus, and are sons of God. Christians are free to enjoy having God's Spirit, and look forward to their inheritance.

Christians are free from obeying the law to be saved; but we're to use our freedom to love others by obeying the law, and to be led by the Spirit instead of the over-desires of our sinful natures.

Talkabout

1. Why do people compare themselves with others?

Investigate

📖 **Read Galatians 5:26 – 6:6**

DICTIONARY

Conceited (5:26): self-centered, always wanting to get honor and value for ourselves.

Live by the Spirit (6:1): living as the Spirit wants.

---

2. Why does being conceited produce "provoking" and "envying" (5:26), do you think?

3. Paul has just told Christians to "keep in step with the Spirit" (v 25)—to remember and apply the gospel of the Son. How will the gospel of justification by faith…
   • make people both humble and bold?

   • remove conceit?

Getting Personal | OPTIONAL

Do you have more of a tendency to provoke or to envy?

One way to know is by how you tend to compare yourself with others. Do you often feel, "I would never, ever do what this person has done; let me think of the ways I would do better"? That's conceit that leads to provocation.

Or do you often think, "I could never, ever accomplish what this person does; I'll dwell on how much better they are"? That's conceit that leads to envy.

When do you struggle with conceit? How will applying the gospel make a difference to your outlook and actions?

4. Instead of the Galatians seeking self-worth in relationships with other Christians, what does Paul tell them to do?
   - 6:1

   - v 2

   - v 3-4

   - v 5

   - v 6

Apply

5. Which of these is your church fellowship good at? Which of these could you do better?

   - How could you, as individuals, make a difference?

Investigate

📖 **Read Galatians 6:7-10**

DICTIONARY

Reaps (v 7): harvests.　　　　　　　**Sows** (v 7): plants.

6. What is the principle of verses 7-8?

Explore More | OPTIONAL

📖 **Read Luke 6:46-49**

Jesus is using an image from the building site, while Paul in Galatians 6 is thinking of the farmer's field.

- But what are the similarities between Jesus' and Paul's words?
- How does Luke 6 help us to understand how we sow to please the Spirit?

7. What does Paul encourage in both verse 9 and verse 10?

- What motivations and priorities does he give for doing this? What does he mean, do you think?

📖 **Read Galatians 6:11-18**

DICTIONARY

Compel (v 12): force.
Flesh (v 13): here, Paul means what people do to their own bodies, i.e. getting circumcised.

Marks of Jesus (v 17): scars that Paul has suffered because of his ministry.

In verse 12, Paul is again talking about his opponents, the false teachers.

8. Why are they telling the Galatian Christians that they must get circumcised to be saved?
   - v 12

   - v 13

   - What does this tell us about what they most want in life? (In other words, what they are trusting and worshiping?)

9. How is real Christianity different (v 14-15)?

10. How do verses 14-15 provide a summary of the whole letter?

Paul finishes by encouraging the Galatians to "follow this rule" (v 16)—that is, to live by the gospel of Christ crucified.

11. What four things does living like this produce (v 16-18)?

• Why are each of these a consequence of loving and living for Jesus, do you think?

Apply

12. How would you sum up the letter of Galatians in a sentence?

• What encouragement and challenge are you taking away from Paul's letter?

Getting Personal | OPTIONAL

"May I never boast except in the cross of our Lord Jesus Christ…" (v 14).

Is the death of Jesus the only thing you are relying on for your standing with God?

"… through which the world has been crucified to me" (v 14).

Can you say that there is nothing in the world that you *have* to have? Are you enjoying the good things in your life, or making them god things that produce anxiety and discontent?

Pray

Use your answers to questions 5 and 12 to guide your prayers.

Galatians

Gospel Matters

Leader's Guide: Introduction

This Leader's Guide includes guidance for every question. It will provide background information and help you if you get stuck. For each session, you'll also find the following:

The Big Idea: The main point of the session, in brief. This is what you should be aiming to have fixed in people's minds by the end of the session!

Summary: An overview of the passage you're reading together.

Optional Extra: Usually this is an introductory activity that ties in with the main theme of the Bible study and is designed to break the ice at the beginning of a session. Or it may be a "homework project" that people can tackle during the week.

Occasionally the Leader's Guide includes an extra follow-up question, printed in *italics*. This doesn't appear in the main study guide but could be a useful add-on to help your group get to the answer or go deeper.

Here are a few key principles to bear in mind as you prepare to lead:

- Don't just read out the answers from the Leader's Guide. Ideally, you want the group to discover these answers from the Bible for themselves.

- Keep drawing people back to the passage you're studying. People may come up with answers based on their experiences or on teaching they've heard in the past, but the point of this study is to listen to God's word itself—so keep directing your group to look at the text.

- Make sure everyone finishes the session knowing how the passage is relevant for them. We do Bible study so that our lives can be changed by what we hear from God's word. So, **Apply** questions aren't just an add-on—they're a vital part of the session.

Finally, remember that your group is unique! You should feel free to use this Good Book Guide in a way that works for them. If they're a quiet bunch, you might want to spend longer on the **Talkabout** question. If they love to get creative, try using mind-mapping or doodling to kick-start some of your discussions. If your time is limited, you can choose to skip **Explore More** or split the whole session into two. Adapt the material in whatever way you think will help your group get the most out of God's word.

1

Gospel Reversed

Galatians 1:1-9

The Big Idea

The biblical gospel of Christ brings us peace and brings God glory. Any change to it completely reverses it, so we should warn those who are adding to it.

Summary

What is striking about the opening to this letter is Paul's frame of mind. The first nine verses are a concerned, strong, direct outburst. His target was a group of teachers who were teaching Gentile Christian converts that they were obliged to keep the Jewish cultural customs of the Law of Moses in order to be truly pleasing to God.

This may not have seemed to the Galatian Christians like a very important departure from the gospel Paul had taught them. But Paul says, in effect, *This is a total repudiation of all that I have taught you!*

That's because a change to the gospel reverses the gospel, and so it is in fact no gospel at all. The gospel is about God's grace in sending his Son, and in calling us to faith in him. God saved us. He accepted us despite our lack of merit, not because we had built up merit. The biblical gospel says, *God accepts us, so we follow him.* Any change to that will cause it to say, *We need to do something, so that God accepts us.*

So the Galatian teachers were not only suggesting a revision of the gospel, but a reversal to it. And Paul reacts with astonishment and anger, at the teachers who deserve condemnation, and at the Christians who are deserting God to follow this false gospel.

The truth of the gospel matters because of what it achieves. The gospel of Christ dying for our sins and rising to rule brings us grace and peace from God, and brings God glory (because it is God alone who achieves our salvation). We, like Paul, need to love this gospel, found in the apostolic teaching and throughout the Bible—we, like him, need strongly to oppose all teaching that reverses it and encourages people to desert God.

Optional Extra

As an icebreaker, play a simple game of "opposites." You say a word, e.g. "day," and group members have to say the opposite of your word as quickly as they can. Include some words which have more than one opposite, e.g. "deep," which could be "high" or "shallow" or "superficial"; "easy," which could be "hard," "difficult," "tricky," "complex" and so on.

This links in with questions 6 and 7; any change to the gospel reverses it, making it the opposite of the true gospel.

Guidance for Questions

1. What makes you surprised or disappointed?

In these verses, we will see what makes Paul both "astonished" and angry (as question 2 outlines). This question introduces this thread, which runs through the study. Allow your group to come up with flippant answers and serious ones. You might like to come back to this question at the end of the study—it links with question 11 and the second Getting Personal box (on page 11 of the Study Guide).

2. As Paul begins his letter, what does his mood seem to be?

- Surprised, not understanding—astonished (v 6). He also seems worried about what is going on in the Galatian church.
- Angry. His language is remarkably strong (especially in v 8-9). He calls down a condemnation on people.

- **What reasons do these verses give for his frame of mind?**
  - v 6-7a: He is astonished because these church members have rapidly turned their backs on knowing the true God (v 6), and are taking hold of a gospel that isn't really a gospel (v 7). They are personally turning their backs on God.
  - v 7b: His anger is prompted by "some people" who, he says, are "pervert[ing] the gospel." (We'll see something of how they're doing this in question 7.) And more indirectly,

his anger is caused by the Galatian Christians' desertion of the God who called them (v 6).

3. How does Paul describe himself in verse 1? What does verse 1 tell us about what he means by this word?

- He calls himself an apostle. The Greek *apostolos* means "sent."
- "Not from men nor by a man" shows the uniqueness of the apostles. They were not chosen by men, but "sent ... by Jesus Christ and God the Father." Paul was commissioned and taught directly by the risen Jesus himself on the road to Damascus (see Acts 9:1-19). The authority which sent him is the same authority that raised Jesus from the dead.

- **OPTIONAL: How does the fact that this letter is written by an apostle change the way we read it?**
  This letter has God's authority. It is not the ideas or views of a Christian teacher, however wise or insightful; it is the teaching of God himself, Father and Son, given through one of his appointed and chosen apostles.

Explore More

- **Read Romans 1:8-10; 1 Corinthians 1:4-7; Ephesians 1:15-17; Philippians 1:3-8; Colossians 1:3-6. What do all these have in common that the beginning of Galatians is lacking?**
  NOTE: To save time, divide your group into pairs, give them one or

two of these passages each, and ask them to report back the main themes of those verses.

Paul follows his greeting with a paragraph of thanksgiving and appreciation for the faith and lives of the people he's writing to.

○ **How do you think Paul would have wanted the Galatian Christians to respond to this omission?**
Presumably to realize the seriousness of the situation, the danger they were in—to sit up and take notice of what Paul has to say.

○ **How does this change how we read the letter to the Galatians?**
It's not going to be a gentle letter! But the truths and challenges in it are ones which we need to hear—and, if we are falling into the same mistakes as the Galatians, we urgently need to change.

- -

4. **Galatians 1:1-5 contains the core of Paul's "gospel," or announcement. So from these verses, what is "the gospel"?**
Your group may say these in a different order.
- We are lost, in need of a rescue (v 4). People are in a helpless condition, unable to recover themselves.
- We need rescuing from "the present evil age" (v 4). We live in a world which is rebelling against its Maker—which leaves us facing the punishment of our Maker.
- Jesus came to rescue us (v 4). He made himself a sacrifice ("gave himself", v 4a) which was substitutionary in nature. The word "for" means "on behalf of" or "in place of." When Jesus becomes our Savior, we are absolutely free from penalty or condemnation.
- God raised Jesus from the dead (v 1), showing that he accepted the work of Christ on our behalf; and showing that Jesus is "Christ" (v 1)—God's appointed, eternal, all-powerful Ruler.

- **Why does this gospel bring people "grace and peace ... from God" (v 3), do you think?**
Grace is God's unmerited favor. The gospel is all about God's favor to us, through his Son. And so this is a message of peace. Jesus' death and resurrection enable us to be at peace with our Maker forever; at peace with ourselves, living life under the rule of God's Son, which is what we were made for; and at peace with others who are living this way.

- **Who gets the glory and praise for the gospel? Why is this fair?**
God alone (v 5). This is right because salvation is all about what God has done—it is his rescue plan, achieved through his Son. We did not ask for it or deserve it—we did not even bring ourselves to understand or respond to it (verses 15-16, which we'll look at in session 2).

5. **Verse 5 is the motivation for everything Paul does. How is this a challenge to us?**

We often live (even as Christians) for our own glory and praise and satisfaction. When we don't live with Jesus as Christ, it is because we care for ourselves more than for God's glory. And we can live with Jesus as Christ with a wrong motivation—for our good rather than to praise him. We can serve God to be noticed, rather than to bring him glory. We can tell others the gospel to feel successful, rather than because we want God to be praised.

Ask your group what would change in their actions if they wanted God to get all the glory, forever. Ask them what they do which is right, but with wrong motivations. Encourage each other to be specific!

6. **Read Galatians 3:1-5. How do some teachers in Galatia seem to have been changing the gospel message?**

They appear to have been suggesting that Christians need to believe the gospel of Christ and observe Jewish (i.e. Old Testament) laws to have the Spirit (v 2) and be saved (v 3) and enjoy God's power and blessing (v 5). They were not saying, *You don't need Jesus. Being good means you'll go to heaven anyway.* They were saying, *Jesus was critical and crucial to getting you saved, of course, but faith in him alone is not enough to grow you into full acceptance with God. You will now have to adopt the full range of the ceremonial and cultural customs that Moses taught.*

7. **What does Paul say about any change to the gospel message (1:6-7)?**

It perverts the gospel (v 7). This word literally means "reverses." If you add anything to Christ (i.e. you need the grace of Christ plus something else) as a requirement for acceptance with God, you completely reverse, totally lose, the gospel. So a slightly amended gospel is, Paul says, "no gospel at all" (v 7).

• **Why is this the case, do you think?**

The word "reverse" is illuminating. Paul reminds these Christians in verse 6 that God "called you [by] the grace of Christ." God called them—they didn't call him. This is the order of the true gospel—God accepts us and then we follow him. But other religious systems have it the other way around: we must give God something (e.g. obedience, law-keeping, ritual observance), and then he accepts us. Any change to the true gospel makes it about what we do for God, rather than what he has done for us. And this is a complete reversal.

8. **What is Paul's attitude to those who "pervert" the gospel (v 8-9)?**

He says they should be "eternally condemned," i.e. rejected by the church, as they will be eternally rejected by God.

○ *OPTIONAL: Who does Paul speak of hypothetically in verse 8, and what does he imagine them doing? What points is he making to us here?*

Paul himself and his mission team, and an angel; preaching a gospel that is different from the one he'd already proclaimed to the Galatian church. Even if an apostle or a heavenly messenger changes the gospel of grace, we must judge that message against the true biblical gospel and reject it, and the apostle/angel who brought it.

- **Think about what we've seen the real gospel is; gives us; and results in for God. Do you think Paul's language here is justified? Why / why not?**

The gospel God has proclaimed through his apostles is true… it brings us God's grace and peace eternally… it results in God getting deserved glory (v 5). So any reversed "gospel" is the opposite: false… leaving us without God's favor, and facing judgment… depriving God of glory (our efforts are what deserve praise, instead of his grace). So Paul is entirely justified to call for judgment on people who encourage others to desert the gospel; who lure people away from the peace of the gospel and back to facing judgment themselves.

9. **When did the Galatians hear the real "gospel of Christ" (v 8)? How does verse 1 give us confidence that this gospel is the true gospel?**

The true gospel is "the one we preached to you"—the apostolic gospel teaching that we find in the Bible, the original "gospel deposit." Our confidence in Paul's message is not, in fact, in Paul himself, but in the one who sent him (v 1). God the Father called him; God the Son appeared to him (Acts 9:3-6). Paul's gospel is God's gospel.

10. **How do people today add to the gospel message?**

Let your group discuss how they see this happening in their own society, or denomination, or hearts. It's worth underlining that Paul condemns any teaching that is not based on the following facts:

- we are too sinful to contribute to our salvation (we need a complete rescue);
- so, we are saved by belief in Jesus' work (the grace of Christ), plus nothing else.

Encourage your group to think about the additions that could creep into your own church, which would be most difficult to spot (and therefore most dangerous).

Here are four examples of current views that deny one or both of these two truths:

- *I am saved through my "surrender to Christ." The feelings my faith produces (which I must maintain) become my savior—not the object of my faith, Christ himself.*
- *I am saved through right doctrine. Intellectual correctness is what saved me.*
- *As long as I am a good person, it doesn't really matter what I*

believe. This sounds extremely open-minded, but it rejects grace. It teaches that I can save myself (it is not humble). And it teaches that bad people have no hope (it is not open).

- *I am saved through following particular rituals or a certain lifestyle.* Some churches regulate dress, dating, how to spend time and money, and so on so tightly that it becomes part of what a "real Christian" is.

11. Why do we sometimes not react to false gospels in the same way as Paul did?

Paul shows us the right reaction: astonishment, concern, and anger—taking the time to write to remind people of what the true gospel is, and warning them about trusting a non-gospel.

There are many reasons why we don't react as Paul did; allow your group to come up with their own ideas. Here are two possible (challenging!) answers:

- Complacency: We don't notice false teaching, or think it matters.
- Selfishness: We don't want to be seen as intolerant, or be known as someone who upsets others, so we keep quiet.

12. Why is the real gospel wonderful?!

This ends the study on a positive note. The best thing we can do for ourselves is to set God's gospel of grace deep into our hearts, to love it and praise God for it, and to remind each other of it. The real gospel is all about what God has done for us; how his Son died in our place to rescue us from our sins and a world under judgment; how God raised his Son to prove he is the Christ and show his acceptance of Christ's sacrifice; and so the real gospel brings eternal grace and peace to those who trust it, and praise to the one who deserves it—God. This is a wonderful gospel to know, and to love!

2

Gospel-Given Unity

Galatians 1:10 - 2:10

The Big Idea
The gospel of grace saves us, changes us, and unites us.

Summary
In this section, Paul points us to the grace of God, who had directly converted him; and to the unity of God's people, who are in fellowship around the gospel truth.

In recounting his conversion, Paul details how he was full of both religious pride and anti-Jesus hatred (1:14, 13). Yet, despite all this, he was not only saved by Christ but also called to be a preacher and leader of the faith. Not only that, but Paul can now see how God was working in him before his conversion (v 15).

Paul is refuting three accusations against him: that his message was derived from others (v 16b-19); that it was the product of his own thinking (v 14-15); that it did not "check out" with the message the Jerusalem church was preaching (v 18-24).

Paul moves on to describe his visit to Jerusalem 14 years later (2:1). The reliability of his message of salvation by grace through faith alone is still the focus. Taking Titus with him presented the church leaders with a flesh-and-blood test case for what makes someone a Christian.

By not requiring him to undergo the Jewish rite of circumcision (v 3), the Jerusalem leaders were stating that no performance, ritual, or behavior is necessary for salvation.

This is the basis of church unity. Unity is vital, as it establishes the reliability of the gospel and enables its spread. Fellowship with Christ means fellowship with those who are in Christ (v 9). And that is the only basis for church unity—those who teach false gospels must be resisted and discredited (v 5).

The Getting Personal sections emphasize the way Paul grew in his faith post-conversion: through solitary time with God (1:17), and through being part of a cohesive community of believers (v 18).

Optional Extra
In pairs, spend a few minutes telling each other about your own journey to faith in Christ, and how God has worked in and through you since then. You could either do this both before the study and afterwards, to see how Paul's testimony helps shape and hone your own; or leave it until after question 4 (or the optional question after question 4, which it is closely related to).

Guidance for Questions

1. **Is church unity important, and why? Is church unity ever a bad thing?** There are no wrong answers at this stage! You might like to return to your

group's ideas when you reach question 9, and analyze them in light of what you've seen in the passage.

2. What does he tell us about...
- **his life before becoming a Christian?**
  - v 13: Paul had done many terrible deeds. He had persecuted Christians, trying to destroy the church. He had been part of the killing of innocent people (see Acts 7:54 – 8:3). He was filled with hate.
  - v 14: Paul had already spent years seeking to live according to the Jewish customs and traditions. He had beaten almost everyone of his own generation at being zealous for moral righteousness. And yet it had not made him "right with God." He was very good at following Jewish laws. He was filled with pride.

- **how he became a Christian?**
  - NOTE: At this point, it is well worth reading the account of Saul/Paul's conversion in Acts 9:1-19.
  - "God … called me by his grace" (Galatians 1:15). He "reveal[ed] his Son in me" (v 16). Paul did not call out to Christ—Christ called out to him. The initiative was Jesus', in appearing to him and speaking to him on the road to Damascus. He had been resisting God—but God worked powerfully in his heart and mind to turn him from a persecutor into a preacher.

- **what he did after becoming a Christian?**
  - v 15-16: God was pleased "to

reveal his Son in me, so that I might preach." When Paul had his personal encounter with the living Christ, he immediately realized that he was being called to show others who Jesus was—to preach.
  - v 17: Paul had solitary time with God. Instead of going to Jerusalem to learn from the other apostles, he went to Arabia, where we assume he learned much from God that he later taught.
  - v 18: He went up to Jerusalem to meet with other Christians.

3. Think about what kind of person Paul had been. What is amazing, and wonderful, about verses 15-16a?
There are several amazing statements in a short space here! Encourage your group to think about each in turn:
- "God, who set me apart from birth": God's sovereign grace was working in Paul's life long before his conversion. God had been shaping and preparing Paul for the things he would call him to do—even his rebellion and failures and flaws were being used by God to bring him to the point of conversion (on the way to arrest Christians) and to be God's instrument to the Gentiles (Acts 9:15). God is at work in his people even before they realize they are his people!
- "called me by his grace": Paul was full of pride and hate—his sins were very deep—yet God still loved him and called him to saving

faith. There is no clearer example than Paul that salvation is by grace alone, not through our moral or religious performance. Even a man such as Paul was not beyond the reach of God's grace.

- "was pleased to reveal his Son in me": Why did God choose and call Paul (or anyone else)? Not because Paul pleased God, but simply because God was pleased to do so.

4. **What kinds of claims about himself does Paul seem to be answering in these verses?**

- That his message came from others, particularly the Christian leaders in Jerusalem—he "did not consult any man, nor did [he] go up to Jerusalem" (Galatians 1:16-17). Paul's gospel is not simply his twist on a humanly taught message.
- That his understanding came through his own reflection and insight. He was "intensely" hostile (v 13) to the church until the moment of his conversion. There was no way that his message could be the result of his own line of thinking.
- That his message was different to the rest of the church's. His gospel "checked out" when he finally visited Jerusalem and Judea (v 18-19, 22-23), and so they "praised God because of me" (v 24).

○ *OPTIONAL: Why has Paul shared his testimony?*

To convince people about the truth of the gospel. He wants to point his hearers to Christ—he does not want to boost his own ego, but to help his friends to understand how gracious God is.

○ *OPTIONAL: How does this guide us about why, when, and how to share our own testimony with others?*

We need to share our own testimonies because Christianity is about our hearts as well as our minds—about how we experience God's love as well as how we understand it. But Paul reminds us here that we should only share our testimony if it is helpful to others. Our testimony must point to the gospel, not leaving people thinking only of the dramatic or risqué details of our past, or of how much we have changed.

5. **What result of a gospel-changed life does verse 10 show us?**

The removal of a man-pleasing spirit—seeking to "win the approval of men." Paul now seeks the approval of God, by serving Christ—without concern for the approval and good opinion of others. And Paul says he cannot do both—a life changed by the gospel means the approval of others no longer sways our actions, and instead pleasing God is what drives us.

6. **When do we find it hard to be a God-pleaser rather than a man-pleaser? Why?**

All sorts of occasions and circumstances! Give your group time to think about and share their own particular challenges in this area. Three which we see in the Scriptures which you might like to mention are:

- 1 Samuel 15:24: King Saul disobeyed God because he was afraid of public opinion and criticism.
- Judges 16:15-21; 1 Kings 11:1-6: Samson and Solomon would rather please their lovers than God.
- Ephesians 6:5-8: Obeying and serving our bosses in the workplace only when they are watching, to gain favor with them (v 6), instead of to please Christ.

- **How will remembering the gospel that saved Paul, and saved us, free us from being driven by man's approval?**

Because now we know that we enjoy God's approval, and can rest assured in his love of us. (You might like to turn forward to Galatians 3:26-27 here—God sees us in the way he sees his Son Jesus.) This frees us from needing to make others' love and approval our primary goal— our identity is secure and our value is found in our relationship with the God of grace. Because God is pleased with us, we are freed and motivated to live in the way which brings him pleasure. If others criticize or ostracize us (as happened to Paul), this does not change our view of who we are or what our purpose is. We know that God loves us, approves of us, and is pleased with us as we live his way.

7. **Why was the Jerusalem leaders' decision about Titus (v 3) so significant?**

Titus was a test case. He was a Greek, i.e. not a Jew. He was uncircumcised. They did not insist on Titus' circumcision before having fellowship with him as a fellow Christian. This was proof that they had accepted Paul's ministry and agreed with his gospel—that it is faith in Christ alone, and not any other performance or ritual, that is necessary for salvation. The acceptance of Titus was a radical public statement that the gospel alone makes us acceptable to God and his people.

- **If they had agreed with the "false brothers" and made the opposite decision, how would "the truth of the gospel" have been lost?**

The church would have been split in two, with neither side accepting the other fully—and one side would have taught that external behavior needed to be added to Christ in order for people to be saved.

8. **What did the apostles in Jerusalem recognize about Paul (v 6-9)?**

- His calling to preach the gospel to Gentiles (v 7), just as Peter had been gifted for preaching to Jews.
- That he was a fellow Christian, who they were united with (v 9). The "right hand of fellowship" showed their acceptance of his gospel message as being the same as theirs. They all shared fellowship with Christ—and therefore with each other.

9. **How does this episode show the importance of pursuing unity within the church?**

Unity within the church enables the mission of the church. It secures and underpins the unchanging biblical gospel message. It isolates and discredits false teachers, who are not included in this unity. The very fact that God gave Paul a revelation (v 2), telling him to go to Jerusalem to establish and show visibly the unity of the church around the gospel, shows the importance of pursuing unity among true Christian believers.

- **How does it show us the limits of pursuing unity? (Verses 4-5 will help.)**

Fellowship with Christ is the sufficient and only basis for fellowship with one another. Paul "did not give in ... for a moment" (v 5) to the "false brothers" (v 4). He made great efforts to be united with those who also believed and taught the gospel—but he would not establish unity at the expense of that gospel.

Explore More

○ **Read Leviticus 23:22 and Deuteronomy 15:7-8. How were God's people in the land of Israel to treat the poor among them?**

Be generous towards them, giving them the opportunity to have food, and to work for their food; to lend to those who were struggling in an "openhanded" way.

○ **Read 1 John 3:16-17 and 2 Corinthians 8:8-15. How are God's people today to treat the poor among us?**

We are to open our hands to the needy as far as there is need—in fact, if God's love is in us, we will act with sacrificial pity toward our brothers and sisters who are in need. Wealth is to be shared very generously between rich and poor.

○ **What example does 2 Corinthians give us?**

The great example is the Lord Jesus (2 Corinthians 8:9), who, in his incarnation, gave up the riches of heaven and "moved in" with the poor, and in his death gave up even his human life in order to share heaven's riches with his people.

○ **Read Matthew 5:43-48 and 25:31-46. What does caring for the poor, and not caring for the poor, show about us?**

Whether we really have justifying faith. The faith which saves shows itself in our service of the poor, the refugee, the sick, and the prisoner.

○ **Why is it right that the apostles made it a priority to agree to "remember the poor" (Galatians 2:10)? How does this challenge you individually, and as a local church?**

Care for the poor, as we have just seen, is a constant in the Bible. The ministry of mercy is a required work of the church, just as is the ministry of mission (v 9), not an optional extra.

10. **In what ways does the gospel give people freedom that normal "earn your salvation" religions don't?**

Allow your group to come up with their own suggestions and ideas. Two main areas you might choose to highlight are…

- cultural: if the false teachers had had their way, an Italian or African could not have become a Christian without becoming culturally Jewish. The gospel gives us the freedom to be ourselves, maintaining our distinctive culture and ethnicity.

- emotional: anyone who believes that our relationship with God is based on keeping up moral behavior is on an endless treadmill of guilt and insecurity. The gospel frees us from thinking that law-keeping is the system of salvation—we obey not in fear and insecurity, hoping to earn our salvation, but in the freedom of gratitude, knowing we are already saved in Christ.

11. **This passage shows us several differences that knowing and loving the true gospel makes. What would these things look like in your life and church community today?**

Encourage your group to come up with specific examples of the outworkings of these gospel-driven changes.

- **1:10**
Enjoying and seeking God's approval, rather than the praise of others.

- **1:24**
Praising God both for our conversion and the news of others coming to saving faith.

- **2:9-10**
Recognizing and being in fellowship with other Christians, including those who have different gifts or callings; remembering the poor among the church worldwide.

3

Gospel: The A-Z

Galatians 2:11-21

The Big Idea

The gospel tells us we are justified by faith alone, not by anything we do—and we must apply this principle to every area of our lives.

Summary

The gospel is the ABC of the Christian life—it is the way we are saved. In this passage, which shockingly begins with two apostles in dispute, Paul lays out the gospel as "justification by faith." We are justified—declared not guilty instead of condemned—only through faith, and not by observing the law. This is the "grace of God" (v 21)—he saves us despite our sin.

But the gospel is actually the A-Z of the Christian life, too. Christians need the gospel as well as non-Christians. It is far more than a ticket to heaven beyond death—it is a radical manifesto for change today.

That is why Paul opposed Peter. In refusing to eat with Gentile believers, he was "not acting in line with the truth of the gospel." In the way he was choosing to eat, he was not reflecting his conviction that all of us are saved by faith alone, and none of our law keeping contributes to this. Living as a Christian means bringing everything in our lives in line with the direction of the gospel.

From verse 17 on, Paul is answering a common objection to the gospel of justification by faith—that it "promotes" sin, because it tells us that our obedience does not change our status with God. This section contains a couple of obscure and difficult statements! There is a brief explanation of verse 18 in the study guide, but since verses 19-21 are so powerful and bear most of the freight of his argument, it isn't critical to understand verse 18.

Paul's point is that while he was obeying the law to try to be justified through obedience, he never really lived for God. He was only obeying him to get a reward— for what he could get from God. Now that he knows that, through Christ's death for him, he is completely assured of acceptance before God, Paul has a new motive for obedience that is far more wholesome and powerful— he wants simply to live for the one "who loved me and gave himself for me."

Optional Extra

If you have a member of your church who is not part of your Bible-study group and who grew up in a culture different from that of your group members, invite them to come and talk about what they found hard (or still find hard) about living in a culture different from the one they were born into; and about the differences between church life in the two cultures.

Ask them what made the transition hard and/or awkward (particularly regarding church life); and what (if anything) people did, or could have done, to make it easier. Then refer back to this as you discuss question 4.

Guidance for Questions

1. **Who needs the gospel, and what difference does it make to them?**

   We tend to think non-Christians need the gospel, as putting their faith in Christ will save them. Paul is going to show that Christians need the gospel too—that it makes a difference to all of life. For now, allow your group to talk about non-Christians and salvation (which are not wrong answers!). If they don't go on to talk about the difference the gospel makes for Christians, come back to this question once you've looked at question 3 and/or question 10.

2. **Peter (Cephas) was one of Jesus' closest friends, who had seen him teach, heal, live, die, and rise. What is surprising about verse 11?**

   Peter had gotten something wrong—something serious enough for Paul to have "opposed him to his face." Here are two apostles disagreeing.

• **What was Peter doing that caused Paul to act like this (v 12-15)?**

   He had withdrawn from eating with Gentile Christians. Under pressure from "certain men," he had begun to "separate himself from the Gentiles" (v 12). Although he himself "live[d] like a Gentile" in how he ate, he was now insisting that Gentile Christians adopt culturally foreign Jewish customs (v 14). Paul calls this hypocritical (v 13)—Peter had begun to hold Gentile converts to a higher standard than he himself maintained! Peter was allowing cultural distinctions to become more important than gospel unity.

3. **How did Paul view Peter's and Barnabas' actions (v 14a)?**

   As "not acting in line with the truth of the gospel."

• **What is significant about this insight, do you think?**

   First, gospel truth has a vast number of implications for all of life. It is our job to bring our lives "in line" with the direction of the gospel—to think out its implications in every area of our lives, and seek to bring our thinking, feeling, and behavior in line.

   Second, Paul points Peter to the gospel. He doesn't simply say to Peter, *You're wrong. Act differently!* He says, *Remember the gospel. Apply the gospel, which graciously welcomes you, to this situation, and graciously welcome others.* We need to be willing to help others change, and to do so by helping them apply the gospel to life.

Explore More

○ *Read Acts 11:1-18. Why did*

Peter originally begin eating with Gentiles?

Because he'd had a vision from heaven (v 5), where he saw a great sheet full of animals forbidden for eating in the Old Testament, and he heard a voice saying, "Kill and eat" (v 7)—because nothing that God has made clean is unclean (v 9). This would have enabled him to eat with people who did not keep the ceremonial food laws of the Old Testament (e.g. Leviticus 11).

○ **What was so significant about this vision (v 18)?**

It showed that through Christ, all believers are made "clean"—whether they keep food laws or not.

○ **How does this make his actions in verse Galatians 2:12 even worse?**

He had seen a vision from heaven (as well as having heard the Lord Jesus' own teaching on this subject, Mark 7:1-23). He had begun to eat with Gentiles, and courageously faced down those who originally disagreed with him (Acts 11:2-4). And now, under pressure from some Judaizing teachers, he had simply stopped living out what he knew to be right. He was being a hypocrite.

4. **What are the ways in which we can insist other Christians act as we do (or even hold them to a higher standard than we hold ourselves)?**

Peter's conduct was a form of legalism, i.e. looking to something besides Christ in order to be acceptable and clean before God. Discuss legalisms you can slip into, such as...

- Peter's sin: nationalism. We can insist that Christians can't be really pleasing to God unless they take on the norms of a particular culture or part of society. Or we can sit next to people from a different ethnic group from us in church, but not "eat" with them—not socialize with them, not share our homes and lives with them.

- class-ism. We can spend time with / invite for dinner only those who are "like us"— middle-class / working-class / have a young family / same line of work etc.

- denominationalism. It is extremely easy to stress our distinctions in order to demonstrate to ourselves and others that our church is "better."

- ability-ism. Very (or even moderately) talented Christians may feel unhappy that people they consider mediocre are part of the church, and an equal part to them.

- **What are the reasons why we find ourselves doing this? (Verse 12 gives us one motivation.)**
  - v 12: Fear of what others think.
  - Comfort: It is simply easier to insist others make themselves like us, and only open our lives and hearts if they are.
  - Pride: Without the gospel rooted in us, we will look for value elsewhere—one way to do this is to find ways in which we are "better" than

others, and so tell them they need to be "like us."

5. In verses 15-16, what does Paul remind Peter about...

• following God's commands?

It cannot "justify" us, or make us "clean" in God's sight. (The context is about Old Testament food laws, which maintained ritual cleanliness among God's people.) "No one" will be saved by observing the law (v 16).

• having faith in Jesus?

Faith in Jesus justifies—even ceremonially clean Jews ("we," v 16) need faith truly to be clean.

• How do these verses shed light on the meaning of the word "justification"?

Paul introduces the principle of "justification by faith" in the middle of a dispute about eating and rules and regulations—in other words, being "clean," So being "justified" is the same as being "clean." Why does Paul switch terms? Because justification has a legal reference, and its opposite is condemnation. Justification reminds us that we are sinners, and without Christ we are completely condemned. But faith in Christ makes us justified (a memorable definition of which is "just as if I hadn't sinned")—God accepts us despite our sin.

6. What is the objection Paul raises to "justification by faith" in verse 17? Why is it a fair point to make?

The objection is that because we can

go on sinning but through faith in Jesus still be justified, Christ actually encourages, or promotes, sin! It's a fair point because being justified by faith alone does remove two motivations for obedience: those of fear and reward.

7. Paul suggests in verse 19 that when he was trying to save himself by obeying the law, he was not able to "live for God." Why is this, do you think?

Because if we obey to save ourselves, all our obedience is selfish. Before becoming a Christian, Paul was being very good, but it was for Paul, not for God—to get a reward from God, not out of love for God himself.

• Now Paul has "died to the law" as the way to save himself, because he knows that Christ and not his own obedience is what saves him. Why does this mean he is now able to truly "live for God"?

Because he knows he is justified, accepted, and loved, he wants simply to give himself to the one who "gave himself for me" (v 20). His acceptance gives him a stronger motive for obeying God.

8. What does verse 20a tell us has happened to a Christian's old, sinful self? Who does God see when he looks at a Christian?

• Our sinful self was crucified with Christ. God treats us exactly as if we died on the cross and paid for every last sin there. We owe nothing—

we have paid it in full on the cross, where Christ paid it for us.

- "I no longer live [i.e. the old Paul] but Christ lives in me." When God looks at the Christian, he sees Christ's perfection and beauty. In a sense, the "I" of the Christian is gone—we are made a new person in Christ.

- **What difference does this make to the way a Christian lives (v 20)?**
We live "by faith in the Son of God, who loved me." The believer lives for, and like, the one who died his death and gave him his perfection. The Christian's "job" is to live "in line" with (or, by faith in) the gospel of Christ, the truth that they are completely loved. The Christian's life is completely reoriented to live in accordance with the gospel, out of love for Jesus our Savior.

9. **Try to put verse 21 into your own words.**
Something like: *As I live life and make decisions, I don't forget God's kindness to me in Jesus and go back to trying to be right with God through being good. If anyone could be saved by being good, Christ's death was pointless.*

10. **From these verses, what is "the truth of the gospel"?**
That through faith in Christ and his death for his people, anyone can be brought from "guilty" to "not guilty" before God (justified); anyone can be made clean before God; anyone can be made right with God. It is through

faith, and only faith, that we are justified completely. This gospel changes the way we think and act as we live "in line" with it.

- **Who needs it? (Remember verses 11-14.)**
Everyone! Even apostles needed to work out how the gospel should change their attitudes and actions.

- **What difference does it make for our lives?**
Complete. The discussion between Paul and Peter teaches us to say of every area of life, every decision we take: what does it mean to live out the principles of the gospel of grace, the gospel of justification through faith, here?

11. **In what areas of life do you find it most difficult to live "in line with the truth of the gospel"?**
Allow your group to think this through—you could give them a minute of quiet to think about themselves, before everyone starts talking. Have ready a couple of examples from your own life. Encourage each other not only to talk about those difficult areas but also to outline what it would look like to "live in line with the gospel."

12. **How might you use the gospel to respond to a Christian saying the following things?**
- **"Jesus saved me, and now I am living his way to continue to earn his forgiveness."**
If you think that you need to earn his

forgiveness, you're saying that you can live in a way which saves yourself—so his death was unnecessary, pointless, and stupid! And, if you are obeying God because you think you'll then be forgiven, you're obeying God because you love yourself and want to be saved, not because you love him and want to please him. Wonderfully though, Jesus has done it all for you—so you can simply ask for forgiveness, and live his way out of love for him. So is Jesus everything to you, or nothing? It can't be half and half.

- **"I get angry when someone cuts me off when I'm driving. It's just so rude."**
Your approval of and any love towards that person is resting on their performance. If they have the same standards as you, you like them; if not, you're angry with them. Remember that in the gospel, the perfect God made imperfect people like you and me right with him. He did not hold our sin against him (which is worse than rudeness toward us!) against us. So, let's apply that gospel to driving. When someone cuts us off, let's think, *I am a worse rule-breaker than them. But I am loved and justified anyway. So I will try to bless that driver, despite their bad manners, just as God blesses me despite my sin.*

- **"Teenagers who become Christians must learn to like long sermons."**
It may be true that it would help Christian teens to listen to lots of Bible-teaching. But they are saved by faith, not by their behavior! Just because some people like long sermons, it doesn't mean all have to. We mustn't insist that others conform to certain cultural ideas or preferences. We can encourage them to make sure they are getting Bible-teaching that is helpful and challenging to them. But they don't have to like long sermons. We're saved by faith, not by sermon-listening!

4

Gospel and Law

Galatians 3:1-25

The Big Idea

Christ's death frees us to live for him and enjoy blessing instead of being cursed, emotionally and eternally.

Summary

Paul is expanding on the central theme of Galatians, which he introduced at the end of chapter 2: that we are not only saved by the gospel; we also grow through the gospel and live by the gospel.

In the section this study looks at, Paul compares the law and faith. His message is simple: faith in Christ saves; law observance cannot. And faith in Christ is the way we continue to live as Christians—we do not begin by faith, and continue by works.

This is what the Galatians have begun to do—and Paul is clear that they are "foolish" and have been "bewitched" (3:1).

Salvation, says Paul, has always been by trusting in God's promise. To understand his argument, it's vital to know the significance of Genesis 12:1-3, where God promises Abraham blessing, and blessing for his family and the whole world. Blessing is enjoying life in God's world under his loving rule—to be given blessing is to be saved.

This promise of blessing is fulfilled in Christ. He took the curse our law-breaking brings—he gave us the blessing his life deserved (Galatians 3:13-14). There is no other way to blessing—we must trust in, and live by, God's promise, not our performance.

In verses 15-25, Paul explains the role of the law. He's answering two objections: If it can't save us, what's the point of the law? And since the law was given to Moses 400 years after the promise was given to Abraham, hasn't the law replaced, or been added to, the promise? No, says Paul: salvation is and has always been based on trusting God's promise. The law is put in place not so we can see how to obey and be blessed, but so we can see that we can't obey, and so search for a Savior—Christ (v 24-25).

The study finishes by briefly considering the place of the law in the Christian life. This theme is returned to in later studies, so don't attempt to fill out a complete answer here!

NOTE: Verses 19-20 are difficult. No one is sure what Paul means or how this fits into the argument. Fortunately, the thrust of his argument and its other supporting points are clear, so it isn't vital to understand verses 19-20.

Optional Extra

Give your group this quiz about US law:
• In Sarasota, Florida, it is illegal to do what while wearing a bathing suit in public? *Sing.*

- In Michigan, a woman must have her husband's permission to do what? *Have her hair cut.*
- In Ohio, it's illegal to sell beer while wearing what? *A Santa outfit.*
- In West Virginia, what must children's breath not smell of in school? *Onions.*
- In Lexington, Kentucky, it's illegal to carry what in your pocket? *An ice-cream cone.*

Guidance for Questions

1. What is the point of God's law?

This is a deceptively hard question! At this stage, don't look for "right" or "wrong" answers—just let your group discuss it. Tell them to keep a look out, as they read Galatians 3, for an answer that Paul gives.

2. What are the answers to Paul's questions in verses 1-5?

- v 1: The Galatians have been "bewitched" (not something anyone wants to hear of themselves!). Paul has already supplied the answer: the "some people" (1:7) who are perverting the gospel.
- v 2: Through believing what they heard, i.e. verse 1. Jesus (a historical man) Christ (God's risen, reigning, promised King), who had been "clearly portrayed as crucified." We receive God the Spirit by trusting Christ, not trusting ourselves.
- v 3: The answer seems to be "yes". Paul is saying, *Having begun by gaining the Spirit through trusting Christ, have you decided to seek to continue in the Spirit-filled Christian life through trusting your own works?*
- v 4: Only the Galatians can answer this. But Paul's point is that, having suffered for turning away from idolatry to trust Christ, they are now turning their backs on Christ—meaning that they suffered for one they are now deserting.
- v 5: The Spirit works among them—even does miracles—as they go on consciously resting in Christ for their acceptability before God and their growth as his people. The Spirit does not work according to the measure of their law-observance.

- **What point is he making to the Galatians?**

  That it was believing in Christ crucified (v 1) that brought God's Spirit to them (v 2) to work among them (v 5). Observing the law had nothing to do with the start, or continuation, of their journey to "the goal" (v 3) of life with God.

3. What do these verses tell us about how we grow as Christians?

We are not just saved by the gospel—we grow as we apply the gospel to every area of life (as we saw in session 3). To progress as a Christian we need continually to repent in the same way as we did when we became Christians—to look to Christ's saving work for us, and abandon any ways in which we are trusting ourselves to complete ourselves in this life, or make ourselves fit for the next. One useful image is that of a window and a mirror. We begin our Christian lives by "looking through a window" to Christ and his saving work on the cross; but often over time we look increasingly in a mirror, focusing on our own efforts and goodness to keep us acceptable to God. But the Christian life is all about "looking through a window" to the cross of Jesus, where we're justified, made righteous, and clothed with Christ (see verses 26-27).

4. How did Abraham (here, Abram) become right with God (v 6)?
By having it credited to him (the word Paul uses means declared, accounted) by God. God responds to Abram's faith by counting him righteous—he treats Abram as though he lives righteously, even though he doesn't.

- **How was this a model for the Galatians—people who were non-Jewish, living 1,500 years after Abraham?**
  - Saving faith is believing the gospel promise. It is not simply that Abraham believed in God, but that he believed what God actually said in his promise to give him a son, and so to bring blessing to him, his family and the world—to "save." Saving faith is more than believing in the existence of God or even assenting to the doctrines and teachings of the Bible in general. It is trust in God to do what he has promised.
  - He shows that saving faith is faith in God's provision, not our

performance. Abraham did not trust in his own ability to have a son (which was, humanly speaking, impossible). He trusted God to do a mighty deed that did not depend on human ability at all. He had faith in God to provide salvation, not in himself to perform his own salvation.

Explore More

○ **Read Genesis 15:1-21. What does Abraham (called Abram here) believe God will do, despite the fact he's nearly 100 years old (v 4-6)?**
Give him a son to inherit all he had, including the promises God made back in 12:1-3.

○ **What does Abraham have to do (v 9-11)?**
Kill a cow, goat, and ram, with a dove and pigeon; cut the animals in half and arrange them opposite each other, creating an aisle or alleyway between the halves.

○ **What passes through this alleyway (v 17)? Who doesn't (v 12)?!**
"A blazing torch"—a sign of God's presence. God passes between the halves. Abraham doesn't—he is in an unnaturally deep sleep!

○ **What is God showing about who will keep this covenant? Why is that good news for imperfect Abraham?**
God will, even if/when Abraham and his descendants don't. God guarantees this relationship—even

if it costs his own death! And, since Abraham is not perfectly obedient, this is good news for him—he can trust in God's promise, not his own performance.

---

5. **What does living by, or relying on, observing the law lead to?**

Galatians 3:10: "A curse," a condemnation. Notice that Paul says in verse 12 that law-observers "live by them [the laws]." To "live by" something means to rely on it for our happiness, fulfillment and confidence.

o *OPTIONAL: How do you think we can know what we are truly living by?*

Ask ourselves questions such as: What is my life based on? What makes me most excited or worried? What, if I lost it, would make me feel as if I had no life left?

• **Why is this, do you think?**

There are two aspects to the curse.

• Theological. If we think we're saved by "goodness," we need to be prepared to really look at what God's law commands as "good." To be saved through the law, we would have to obey the law wholly, and that can't be done. Law-keeping-for-salvation leaves us "under a curse"—condemned eternally as lawbreakers.

• Emotional. Salvation through works will lead to profound anxiety and insecurity, because you can never be

sure you are living up to your standards sufficiently (and certainly not that you're living up to God's standards). You're sensitive to criticism, envious of and intimidated by others who outshine you, devastated or in denial about your flaws. So you become nervous and timid (because you're unsure of where you stand) or boastful and complacent (because you're trying to ignore the fact you're unsure of where you stand!) Either way, you live with a sense of curse and condemnation.

o *OPTIONAL: This second "curse" is harder to draw out. You may need to ask: How is it an emotional curse day to day, as well as a curse under God eternally?*

6. **If verse 10 is true, how can God credit us as righteous without being unjust (v 13)?**

In verse 10 Paul quotes Deuteronomy 27:26—everyone is required to keep all the law to avoid condemnation. How can we avoid the curse? Because of what Jesus did. He "became a curse for us" when he was "hung on a tree" (NIV84). (In the Old Testament, an executed person was hung on a tree or pole as a symbol of divine rejection.) When Christ hung on his cross, he was experiencing the curse of divine rejection. And so he "redeemed us" (freed us) from the curse of our law-breaking by taking it "for" (on behalf of, in place of) us. Our sins have been punished—the deserved curse has been taken—but by Christ, standing in our place.

- **What does trusting in Christ's death give us (v 14)? Why is this exciting?**
  - Blessing. Christ, through the perfect obedience of his law-keeping life, had earned blessing, not condemnation. He redeemed us "in order that the blessing" could come to us through him.
  - The Spirit. As God's Spirit lived with and in the man Jesus, so now he lives in those who have faith in him.

  Our salvation is much more than forgiveness. We do not simply have our slate wiped clean; we become perfect in God's sight. Which is a wonderfully exciting truth!

7. **How does Paul answer this objection (v 15-18)?**

   Paul takes a human contract ("covenant"), like a legal will, as an example. Human contracts are difficult or impossible to break. Once a will is made, we consider it binding, no matter what then happens. So "the law … does not … do away with the promise" (v 17). The law of Moses cannot turn God's promise to Abraham into something other than what it is—a promise. If the law of Moses had been intended for us to save ourselves by law-keeping, then salvation "no longer depends on the promise" (v 18). God would have changed his mind and decided that salvation could be about our performance, not his promise. He would

have gone back on his binding word to Abraham.

This is complicated! To summarize: if the law of Moses was the way to be saved, the promise to Abraham wouldn't have been a real promise. Since it was a promise, the law of Moses must have a different purpose.

8. **What doesn't the law achieve (v 21)?**

   It can't "impart life." It cannot give us the power to become, or stay, righteous.

- **What does the law achieve (v 22-23)?**

  It shows us our sin, and that we are a prisoner of sin—unable to free or cure ourselves. The law shows us that we do not just fall short of God's will, but that we are completely under sin's power. As we look at the law and try to obey it, and find that we can't, however hard we try, we see that we cannot be our own savior.

- **So, what is the point of the law (v 24-25)?!**

  To lead us to Christ. The main point of the law is to show us that we need a savior—to teach us to look for, and find, and trust, Jesus Christ. Once we put our faith in Christ and are completely justified and blessed, we no longer need the tutelage of the law—we have learned what it is there to teach us.

9. **"We are no longer under the supervision of the law" (NIV84).**

Does this mean Christians shouldn't be concerned about obeying the law, do you think? Why / why not? (Hint: 2:19-20 might help you here.)

We shouldn't worry about obeying the law in order to be saved—we cannot manage it, and Christ has removed our need to even attempt it. But this does not mean we no longer have to obey God's law! When we grasp salvation-through-promise, our hearts are filled with gratitude—we want to please our Savior by living the way he wants. And we want to be like our Savior, living as he did. As Paul says in 2:20: "Christ lives in me." The way to do this is by obeying the law—this is how we can "live for God" (v 19).

10. **Why do people need to know that God is a God who has laws, before they can understand why Jesus' death is good news?**

Unless we see how helpless and profoundly sinful we are, the message of salvation will not be exhilarating and liberating. Unless we know how big our debt is, we cannot have any idea of how great Christ's payment was. If we do not think that we are all that bad, we won't humbly accept, and be changed by, grace.

11. **How might a professing Christian believer end up coming under the curse of law-observance without realizing it?**

By forgetting that we don't just start the Christian life through being redeemed and blessed by Christ; we continue in it in the same way. It's easy to begin the Christian life trusting in grace, but end up thinking we must perform, or keep particular rules, to continue to be saved. E.g. not sinning in certain ways; improving our obedience; church attendance; becoming like other Christians we know.

At the least, this will lead to the emotional curse of anxiety or even despair, because we'll lose assurance of God's favor to us. It can lead to a brittle pride, because we're basing our view of ourselves on our own performance. And it can even leave us facing the legal divine curse, because if we really are relying on our own efforts as well as Christ's death, we are living by law (3:12), and so are "under a curse" (v 10), as unredeemed law-breakers.

• **What would you say to someone who has done this?**

Let your group discuss this. It will depend to an extent on the individual. Some may need reassuring that Christ died for all their sins. Others may need challenging about the proud self-sufficiency that has led them to add their works to Christ's saving work.

5

Gospel Adoption
Galatians 3:26 - 4:31

The Big Idea

Christians are free, because we are sons of God through faith in Christ. Every other religious system is enslaving.

Summary

Galatians 3:26-29 is the climax of all Paul has said so far in the letter. If Jesus as "the Seed" (3:19) gets all of Abraham's promised blessings, then anyone, Jew or Gentile, who belongs to Christ through faith becomes an heir to those promises. So all Christians are "sons of God" (v 26, NIV84—see note on question 2). When God looks at us, he sees his perfect Son (v 27). We are given all that belongs to the Lord Jesus. Through the Son, we become God's sons legally (4:4-5); and through the Spirit, we experience the joy of living as his children (v 6-7).

But the Galatians, who had once worshiped pagan idols (v 8), are now being persuaded that they need to keep the Old Testament law to be saved. Having turned from their own efforts, they are now "turning back" to them again (v 9), in a different guise. Paul is saying that earning one's own salvation through keeping the Bible's law is just as much a reliance on our own effort, and an enslavement to an idol, as "pagan" religion. In both systems, we rely on our own efforts to serve a false god in order to know security and satisfaction.

To summarize, Paul uses Abraham's two sons, and their mothers, "figuratively" (v 24). Hagar was a slave who represents the slavery of trying to be saved by works (v 25). Sarah was a freewoman, and represents being saved through faith in God.

Paul is saying to the Galatians, and to us, that we will either have ourselves as our savior, or we will have Christ. The first cannot save, and leads to slavery. The second brings us to "the Jerusalem that is above … free" (v 26).

Optional Extra

Before the meeting, ask group members to draw out and bring in their family trees.

You could talk about whether anyone would like to change their family tree; and if they had to swap their family tree for a famous person's one, whose would they go for?

This study is all about family trees, in a way. Faith in Christ means we're adopted into God's family; and faith in Christ means we are, figuratively, part of Sarah's "free" family, rather than Hagar's "slave" one.

Guidance for Questions

1. **If you asked 100 people what the difference is between Christianity**

and other religions, what answers do you think you would get?

Some possibilities:

- There is no difference; they are all ways to God (or, none of them are!).
- Christianity is a Western cultural idea, imposed on other societies. Other religions are other cultural expressions.
- Christianity is different because it teaches that Jesus is God, and other religions disagree with this.

- **What would you say is the difference (if any)?**

This brings the question closer to home. Many Christians wouldn't be confident to explain what makes their faith distinct. Some would want to go into every detail of difference, but wouldn't be sure what the main, overriding differences are. You could return to this after question 10.

2. **Who is a child (or son—see NIV84) of God, and why (3:26-27)?**

Anyone who has faith in Christ (v 26). Baptism (v 27) is a sign of that faith—but it's through faith alone that we are adopted by God into his family as his sons. We are seen as sons because we have "clothed" ourselves with Christ, God's Son (v 27). To say that Christ is our clothing is to say that in God's sight we are loved because of Jesus' work and salvation.

NOTE: Many may take offence at using the masculine word "sons" to refer to all Christians, male and female. But translating it "children" (as the 2011 update to the NIV does)

misses the meaning. In most ancient cultures, daughters could not inherit property. "Son" therefore meant "legal heir"—the one who would inherit everything the father had to give. The gospel tells us we are all sons—inheritors—in Christ.

Similarly, the Bible describes all Christians together as the "bride of Christ" (Revelation 21:2). God is evenhanded in his gender- specific metaphors; it is wonderful for Christian women to be sons of God, and for Christian men to be the bride!

3. **Why is it wonderful to be a son of God?**

- **3:29**

God's sons are "heirs according to the promise." All that was promised to Abraham—the blessing of salvation (as we saw in the last study) is given to a believer, through faith in the Seed, Christ (see verse 16).

- **4:1-5, 7**

When Christ redeemed his people from the law, removing all penalty or debt, God's people who had faith in the promise "came of age". Before, God's people had been like young children, promised much in the future but actually still slaves (v 1). Jesus gives us the full rights of sons. He gave us "sonship"—this refers to a Roman process whereby a wealthy man could adopt one of his servants as his son. Verse 7 sums it up: it's wonderful to be a son because it means we are not a slave. Through Jesus, we are legal heirs of all God has to give.

- **4:6**

  We have an intimate relationship with the Creator of the cosmos. We can cry out "Father" and, perhaps even more amazingly, "Abba," which means "Dad," "Papa," "Daddy." We can rest totally assured of God's fatherly love for us—it rests not on what we do, but who we are in his sight. And we can draw wonderfully near to God in prayer.

  It is worth pausing here to meditate on this, and pray in thanks that we have this relationship with the God who made and controls everything.

- *OPTIONAL: What is Paul saying in 3:28?*

  We are all "one." Any two people who are Christians have more in common with each other than with non-Christians of their own sex, social status, or race.

  NOTE: This does not mean that we do not keep our distinct culture. (One of the main points of the book is that Greek Christians don't need to become Jewish Christians!) Nor does it mean there should be no distinctions between male and female, or employer and employee, in the way we live (see Ephesians 5:21-33; 6:5-9).

- *OPTIONAL: How does this radical unity flow from verse 26?*

  Because the amazing privilege of sonship surpasses the greatest earthly advantages, whether merited or inherited. And because we know we are sons by grace, through faith,

our pride in who we are (ultimately, sinners) is removed.

4. **What is the connection between the work of the Son and the Spirit (v 4-7)?**

   The Son's purpose was to secure for us the objective legal status of sonship. Sonship is about faith, not feelings.

   The Spirit's purpose, by contrast, is to secure for us the experience of sonship. "Because [we] are his sons" (v 6), through Christ's redeeming work, we receive the Spirit to enable us to enjoy that relationship. The Spirit brings the subjective enjoyment of the objective standing we have through the Son.

5. **When we don't feel joyful as Christians, or loved by God, what do we need to do?**

   We need to remember our legal standing before God as his adopted sons, given to us by his Son, Jesus. This is true regardless of our feelings (3:26-27). As we reflect on who we are to God, through Christ, the Spirit will begin to make these truths thrilling and healing, enabling us to feel what is already true of us.

   So, to enjoy our sonship, we need to...

   - put significant time aside to study the work of the Son, asking the Spirit to make it real and exciting to us.
   - "call out" to our Father, regularly, throughout our day. We need to make sure we experience and enjoy

the blessing of knowing God as Father. This will mean asking ourselves, "Am I acting like a slave who is afraid of God or like a child who is assured of my Father's love?"

6. **But what does Paul say they're turning to in verses 8-10?**

"Weak and miserable principles" (v 9, NIV84)—the view that we must save ourselves in some way.

- **What is the implication of what Paul's saying here?**

Crucially, he says they are in danger of "turning back" (v 9)—to be enslaved "all over again". Paul is saying that trying to earn your own salvation through scrupulous Bible morality and religion is just as much enslavement to idols as outright pagan false-god worship. Both are ways of trying to save yourself, through keeping rules or by securing the favor of an idol.

Explore More

○ **How does Paul describe his relationship with these Galatians?**

○ *v 13-14*

He preached the gospel to them. He was ill, but despite this "trial" for them (v 14), the Galatians did not scorn him, but treated him like an angel.

○ *v 15-16*

Now there has been a change. There is a suspicion that he is their "enemy" (v 16), without their best interests at heart. There is no joy in the relationship (v 15).

○ **How does his ministry differ from that of the false teachers (v 16-20)...**

○ **in its goal?**

The false teachers want the Galatians to be "zealous" for them (v 17); Paul wants "Christ [to be] formed in you (v 19). The false teachers want loyalty and popularity; Paul wants Christ-likeness.

○ **in its means?**

The false teachers are "zealous to win you over"—they will say what people want to hear in order to get their loyalty (see 2 Timothy 4:3-4). Paul is willing to risk being seen as an "enemy" to tell them "the truth" (Galatians 4:16). He loves them enough to say hard things.

○ **What does this teach us about true, faithful gospel ministry?**

- *It can involve unpopularity because of the truth (v 16).*
- *It can be heartbreaking (v 19).*
- *It urges people to become like Christ (v 19).*
- *It wants to be gentle in tone but is prepared to say hard things (v 20, 16).*

---

7. **Read Genesis 16:1-4; 18:10-14; 21:1-10. What are the differences between the births of these two sons?**

Abraham had two sons—Ishmael and Isaac—by two different women. Hagar, the slave of his wife Sarah, bore him Ishmael, while Sarah bore him Isaac. Ishmael was conceived in the ordinary way ("according to the flesh," Galatians 4:23)—Abraham slept with a young, fertile woman, and she became pregnant. Isaac, though, "was born as the result of a divine promise"—Sarah was a barren woman and very old, and so it took an extraordinary supernatural act of God for a son to come to Abraham through her.

- **How much faith did Abraham need to have a son with Hagar? How much did he need to have a son with Sarah?**
  - With Hagar, none—he could rely on his own ability (and hers). He could gain a son by his own effort.
  - With Sarah, great faith—he had to rely on God's grace, on God doing the humanly impossible. He could only trust and wait for God to work.

8. **What does Paul say each mother represents (Galatians 4:24-26)? Why?**

Hagar represents the law covenant of Sinai and the earthly city of Jerusalem, who are "in slavery" (v 25—because the great majority of them had not accepted Christ). Hagar represents seeking to be saved by our own efforts.

Sarah represents the grace that comes from God through his Son, and therefore members of "the Jerusalem that is above" (v 26): heaven. Sarah trusted God's promise and represents those who trust God to save them by his work in Christ.

- **The residents of Jerusalem would have thought of Sarah as their mother, and Hagar as the mother of unrighteous Gentiles. Why does this give extra force to what Paul says here?**

Paul swaps the family trees over! The approach of the Jewish false teachers in the church is the same as Abraham's as he slept with Hagar, trusting his own efforts. They are slaves, just as she was—to the anxieties, guilt, and inadequacy of seeking works-righteousness.

Conversely, the Gentile Christians are descendants of Sarah! They are the real sons of Isaac—because they rely on the supernatural power of God to fulfill his promises, rather than their own ability.

9. **What is Paul saying the Galatians should expect (v 28-29)?**

To be persecuted (if they trust Christ) by those who are law-keepers. He flatly states that the children of the slave will always persecute the children of the free woman.

○ *OPTIONAL: How is verse 31 a summary of the whole thrust of Paul's argument from 3:1 onwards?*
Paul is saying to these Gentile Christians: "You are the free ones; they are the slaves. You are already Abraham's true children, free and part of the heavenly Jerusalem. Slavery is trying, and failing, to save yourself. Freedom is knowing that Christ has done it all for you. Don't give up your freedom!" And this has been his point since 3:1.

Christ has taken our curse and given us his sonship—there is nothing we need or could have which is not found in him. We must simply rely on him to give us everything, and not begin to rely on ourselves to get these things.

10. **Why do both non-religious and religious people need the gospel?**

Everyone is trying to earn their salvation— significance, security, satisfaction—by worshiping something. We all need a sense of worth or value. So we worship something to give us this sense of value.

- Non-religious people worship something. But these things control us and then disappoint us if we gain them or devastate us if we lose them.
- Religious (or moral) people are trying to save themselves by being "good". They trust their own law-keeping to put God in their debt, and to give them the life they want (possibly simply through feeling proud about being good people). Jesus may be our example or helper—but we think we are our own savior.

Both non-religious and religious people can't earn what they're seeking. They need the gospel of grace to give them what they cannot find, and cannot earn.

- **Why do religious people persecute gospel people (v 29), do you think?**

Because the gospel is more threatening to religious people than to non-religious people. Religious people are very touchy and nervous about their standing with God. Their insecurity makes them hostile to the gospel, which insists that their best deeds are useless before God.

6

Gospel Freedom, Gospel Fruit

Galatians 5:1-25

The Big Idea

The gospel frees us to love God and others; his Spirit helps us live out the gospel and battle with our sinful natures.

Summary

In Galatians 5:1, Paul reintroduces the idea of Christian freedom that he mentioned in 2:4. Jesus has set us free from the burden of trying to gain justification by law-keeping, and from the crushing disappointment of worshiping idols, which cannot deliver. And Christians need to "stand firm" in this freedom.

This means not losing our freedom by turning back to rule-keeping or rule-breaking as a way of life; it also means not abusing our freedom. The true expressions of faith are certainty about our future (5:5) and love for God and others in the present (v 6).

So Christian freedom does not mean we will disobey God. In fact, the gospel frees us to lovingly obey him, and to do so by loving others (v 14), because we don't obey out of fear, or do things for others because we need something. God has already given us value and security in the gospel. And the gospel of Christ's love for us motivates us to obey, as we've already seen in these studies.

As free children of God, Paul calls the Galatians to live not by the law but by the Spirit (v 16, 18). Paul talks of, literally, the "over-desires" of the sinful nature (v 16-17)—desiring a good thing as a god thing, treating it as what we most need, and doing anything to get or maintain it. Christians are to battle against these over-desires, and enable the Spirit to grow gospel fruit in their character.

So Paul calls them to do two things: to stand firm in their gospel freedom, knowing they have everything they need in Christ; and to battle their sinful natures, so the Spirit can work to make them more like Christ, reflecting the one who has saved them and freed them to love God and others.

Optional Extra

Conduct a blind tasting test with a variety of fruits: some common, some rarer and harder to guess! Blindfold each group member and give them a piece of each fruit to see if they can guess what it is.

Guidance for Questions

1. **Why does a child obey his or her parents?**

   There is more than one answer to this question! Think about…

   • fear: because they'll be punished if they don't.

81

- duty: it's the downside of being looked after!
- reward: to earn their parent's love (or a treat like candy). This is actually similar to fear. Obedience-through-fear is about avoiding something bad; obedience-for-reward is about gaining something good.
- example: it's how other children treat their parents.
- love: because they want to please people who they know have done much for them, and who already love them. If you don't know your parents love you already, regardless of your obedience, you cannot act out of love. You will be acting out of fear or hope of reward: to earn love, or to not lose love, rather than as a response to the love you have and cannot lose.

2. What has Christ done (v 1)?
"Set us free." Everything about the Christian gospel is freedom.

- **What should be our response to this?**
"Stand firm." This freedom can be lost (the whole letter is about this danger). Stand firm is a military term, meaning keep alert, be strong, resist attack. Christians need to be vigilant, remembering they are free and enjoying that freedom, rather than becoming "burdened" by a "yoke of slavery"—thinking they need to obey God in order to be saved, to be his children.

○ *OPTIONAL: What does Paul warn the Galatians about in verses 2-4?*
Against deciding that justification requires Christ-plus-obedience. This means they would be relying on the law (v 3), and so would only be saved through obeying all the law. And so they would lose Christ and the justification he gives (v 4); they would have "fallen away from grace."

○ *OPTIONAL: Paul might seem to be saying that real Christians can lose their salvation in verse 4. How does verse 10 help us to understand what he is saying?*
Christians are people who know they are justified through faith in Christ. And so Paul says in verse 10 that he is confident that the Galatians will not, ultimately, turn their back on the gospel. So he clearly believes they are real Christians—confused and struggling, but people who do trust Christ alone. Their positive response to his warning will show they do believe the gospel in their hearts. A negative response would show they had not ever really grasped the gospel of salvation by faith in Christ alone.

3. What are the expressions of real saving faith—and what aren't (v 5-6)?
- "Eagerly await[ing] … the righteousness for which we hope." Point out to your group that "hope" in the Bible is not a weak wish that something could happen—it is to have a powerful certainty and assurance of something. A Christian

has a deep conviction about the future—that we will be right with God for eternity. The certainty of our future with God, based not on our performance but on Christ's, is a fruit of the gospel.

- Love. If we have faith in Christ, and therefore certain hope for our future, we will have a heart sloshing over with love. Love is the outworking of true faith. We'll look more at this in question 4.
- Neither circumcision (outward religion) nor uncircumcision (not going through religious ceremonies) are "of any value" in showing that we are, or aren't, saved.

4. **What should they use their gospel freedom to do (v 13-14)?**

Serve others (v 13), i.e. everyone ("neighbor," v 14), in love.

- **How does the gospel free us truly to love God and others, do you think?**

Before believing the gospel, someone will only serve God to earn his love or reward, or for fear of what he will do if they don't. And they will only serve others for what others can bring them (friendship, reputation, sense of identity, so others will be nice back). Without the gospel, we can't love God for himself, or love others. But in the gospel, we find that God already loves us and has given us all we need. So we can love him truly, and serve him for who he is, out of love for him. And since in the gospel we have all we need, we don't need to seek it in others. We can simply love them and serve them, without needing, seeking, or demanding anything at all in return.

- **How does it motivate us to love God and others, do you think?**

Because Christ has set us free at such cost, we will gratefully want to please him. Pleasing him will be our goal in how we live. The gospel shows us not only that God has the right to demand obedience as our Creator; he also deserves our loving obedience as our Redeemer. So the gospel motivates us to love God—and, since he calls us to love others as ourselves (verse 14, quoting Leviticus 19:18), we will be motivated to please him by serving others sacrificially. We obey God not out of fear or for reward, but out of love in response to his love for us. (You might like to refer back to question 1 at this point.)

5. **How might we obey God, but for wrong or inadequate reasons?**

Your answers to question 1 will help here. It is possible to serve God but be motivated by a wrong view of how God relates to us as his people:

- Fear: because we don't want to go to hell.
- Duty: because he is God, so we have to do what he says.
- Reward: because we want to go to heaven.
- Debt-repayment: because we owe him after what he did for us. Our obedience is a way of trying to pay him back.

Of course, we can also serve him out of a wrong view of ourselves:

- Value: to make ourselves feel worthwhile.
- Reputation: to cause others to respect and praise us.

○ *OPTIONAL: How does the gospel undermine or transform these motivations?*

Explore More

○ *Read Philippians 3:12-14; Hebrews 12:1-3. What do these passages tell us about how to keep running the Christian race?*

- *Philippians 3: "Press on" (v 12) by not settling for what we have now (v 13a) or worrying about what has already happened (v 13b), but instead straining towards heaven. We're to live leaning forwards.*
- *Hebrews 12: Get rid of sin, which threatens to trip us up (v 1); fix our eyes on Jesus, who is both the object of our faith, and our great example in living by faith (v 2); don't get weary when we face opposition (v 3).*

○ *How do they motivate us to keep running?*

- *Philippians 3: There is a great prize ahead of us, kept in heaven for when our race is finished.*
- *Hebrews 12: Many have run the race before us (the "great cloud of witnesses" refers back to the heroes of faith in Hebrews 11); like Jesus, we will know eternal joy*

beyond the scorn we face in this world.

---

6. What is going on inside every Christian (v 16-17)?

A conflict, or battle, between the Spirit—a believer's Spirit-renewed and indwelled heart—and the "sinful nature." "Sinful nature" means the sin-desiring aspect of our whole being. Before someone becomes a Christian, they have only a sinful nature. Then the Spirit enters them and changes their heart, and the conflict begins. Now (v 17) the believer desires to live for God (to "walk by the Spirit" v 16), yet finds himself following his sinful nature, the "desires of the flesh." It is a fierce conflict!

- **What is encouraging about this truth? What is challenging?**
  - Christians often become demoralized as they find themselves doing what they don't really want to do—sinning. Or as they feel themselves conflicted and pulled in two directions—sometimes sinning, sometimes living God's way. Paul says to the internally battling Christian, *This is the Christian life! The battle is not a sign that something is wrong, but that something is right—the Spirit is at work.* And the end of verse 17 is full of affirmation. The real us—the eternal us—is not the sinful nature, but the Spirit-led person. Even when we are falling into sin, we can say, *This is not the real me: not who*

I really am or what I really want. I am God's, and I want him and his will.

- The challenge is never to expect our lives to be easy. Every day, we must seek to follow the Spirit. We will never get beyond the battle, and we can never give up the struggle. And we never have to sin—we can always choose to follow the Spirit's promptings and desires.

7. What does this tell us about how our sinful nature works?

The main problem is not that we desire bad things, but that we over-desire good things. The sinful nature turns something good into a god, claiming we need it to be truly ourselves: to know real security, significance, or satisfaction. These over-desires are sinful because they deny that God is who we need. We all have the experience of feeling that we must have something, and find ourselves doing anything—even things we know to be wrong—to get it. That is an over-desire—the work of our sinful nature.

8. Look at the "acts of the sinful nature" in verses 19-21. Pick out two or three, and think about how they are consequences of "over-desire."

Take the first one, sexual immorality, as an example. My sinful nature over-desires sexual pleasure. It tells me that I must have it if I am to be really satisfied as a person. I will be significant if I can think of myself as sexually active/expert. It makes

sex—a good, created thing—into my god. Since I need it, I am prepared to give up my marriage vows, and steal the purity of another person, in order to have sex—sexual immorality.

Some of these acts are outworkings of over-desiring something else; for instance, I over-desire a bigger house. I become jealous of my friend who already has one; I am driven not by unselfish love for others, but by selfish ambition, which means I put others down; when my offer on my dream house is rejected, I suffer a fit of rage; and so on.

9. Pick a couple of the aspects of the fruit of the Spirit from verses 22-23. How are these things products of believing the gospel? How are they aspects of serving others in love?

For example:

- Joy: I already have everything I need in knowing God as my Father, for today and forever. I am significant because I am his child, satisfied by having him, and secure in his love. When I lose (or gain) good things which the world offers, I have a deep-down joy which cannot be shaken or destroyed, because it rests on who I am to God and what I have in him, not on who I am or what I have in the world.

- Gentleness: God is pleased with me; I don't need to win others' approval, or put others down. I am heading for God's kingdom; I don't need to tread on others to get ahead in life. God sees and knows me; I don't need constantly to be noticed.

Whereas the sinful nature's work is all selfish and me-centered, all these aspects of the Spirit's fruit allow us to love one another. For example, Spirit-grown joy takes delight in good things happening to others (rather than being envious); and it encourages joy and contentment in others, instead of promoting thanklessness.

10. **What is our part in producing these qualities? What is the Spirit's part (v 18, 22, 25)?**

We work to be "led by the Spirit" and to "keep in step" with him. As we do so, the Spirit works in us to produce and grow this fruit in us. We work as God works—God works as we work (see Philippians 2:12-13). It's helpful to think about the two mistakes that lie on either side:

- All Spirit, no effort on my part—we must keep in step with him, battling the sinful nature.
- All me, no Spirit—it is the Spirit who grows fruit, not me. If I think it is up to me, I will grow proud or envious, and not know peace—which is the opposite of the Spirit's work.

11. **Which of the acts of the sinful nature are most common, and most acceptable, in your culture?**

This is an opportunity to think about which of those things in Galatians 5:19-21 your group is most likely to do without noticing; or to find ready-made excuses for doing; or

to seem most strange for refusing to join in with.

12. **Which aspects of the fruit of the Spirit are least noticed and celebrated within your church?**

Churches tend to celebrate and praise some aspects of the Spirit's fruit more than others—or even, sadly, to recognize and exalt only gifts (such as teaching or speaking in tongues), which God gives only to some Christians, instead of encouraging and noticing the fruit, which the Lord wants all Christians to grow as they live by the Spirit.

- **What would these look like in action?**

Encourage your group to think about specific ways this fruit would show in people's attitudes and actions, both towards God and others. It may be that people in your group suddenly realize that others in your church have been, unnoticed, growing this fruit— prompting thanksgiving to God and encouragement of those individuals.

7

The Gospel Is Enough
Galatians 5:26 - 6:18

The Big Idea

Christ is all we need. Our identity should not come from what others are doing, or what others think of us, but from who we are in Christ.

Summary

The first half of this study (5:26 – 6:6) is bristling with practical principles for relating to others. But (as we should be used to in Galatians by now!) Paul points to the gospel of Christ as the liberator and motivator for truly unselfish relationships. Only the gospel can prevent us feeling superior and/or inferior as we compare ourselves with others (5:26); instead, we find ourselves both humbled and emboldened, and we look at our own responsibility to serve God with what he has given us, rather than at others and how they are doing (6:4).

The second half is in many ways a summary of the whole letter—especially verses 14-15. Having encouraged the Galatian church once more to live to please the Spirit rather than the sinful nature (v 8) by doing good to others (v 9-10), Paul compares false religion with true Christianity.

The false teachers are seeking self-salvation (security, acceptance, status) through their religious performance (v 12-13); Paul is trusting in Christ and his death alone (v 14). It is not about what

he does, but about what Christ has done and is doing for him (v 15). So, despite the suffering he goes through for his faith and mission (v 17), he—like all true Christians—knows peace, mercy, and grace (v 16, 18). It is Paul's final invitation to the Galatians to live by the gospel of Christ. The gospel is enough—all we need for a loving, secure, joyful relationship with God, and a similar relationship with those around us.

Optional Extra

This session's optional extra is designed to be used at the end of this study. You can find it on page 92.

Guidance for Questions

1. **Why do people compare themselves with others?**

   There are no wrong answers to this! It's likely that the conclusion will be that we compare ourselves with others to see how we're doing—how we measure up. We want to know how to be successful and fulfilled, and we find out how to be these things by looking at what others have or strive for. Then we strive for those things, and work out if we have enough of them by comparing ourselves with others.

2. **Why does being conceited produce "provoking" and "envying" (5:26), do you think?**

Because, if we're conceited, we're insecure, and so we are fixated on comparing ourselves with others. We then either feel superior—and want others to notice, thereby provoking others to annoyance, despair, confrontation—or we feel inferior—and are devastated, envying those with more than us, or who seem better than us.

3. **Paul has just told Christians to "keep in step with the Spirit" (v 25)—to remember and apply the gospel of the Son. How will the gospel of justification by faith…**

• **make people both humble and bold?**

The gospel tells people they are sinners, who cannot earn what they most need—eternal blessed life. This is humbling!

But the gospel also tells someone that, if they have faith in Christ, they are loved and honored in the only eyes in the universe that really count. Without the gospel, I will either be bold but not humble (if I'm feeling superior) or humble but not bold (if I'm feeling inferior)—or I'll swing wildly between the two. But the gospel gives a humility and a boldness that don't eat each other up, but can increase together.

• **remove conceit?**

The gospel creates a whole new self-image. We don't need to secure honor from others, since we are loved and approved of by God himself. We don't need to compare ourselves to others to find out how to be blessed, or to find out how blessed we are—we are completely and eternally given all we need in Christ.

4. **Instead of the Galatians seeking self-worth in relationships with other Christians, what does Paul tell them to do?**

• **6:1**
  • Don't overlook someone being "caught in" (i.e. falling into a pattern of) a particular sin. (This doesn't mean be quick to criticize—see 1 Corinthians 13:5; Luke 6:41-42).
  • Seek to "restore" that person. The Greek word means to put a dislocated bone back in place—so restoration may involve pain, but it is for the good of both the person and the whole church body.
  • Do it "gently," by watching yourself carefully. We mustn't think we are not susceptible to temptation ourselves. Remembering that we too could be caught will keep us humble in restoration, not superior.

• **v 2**

"Carry each other's burdens"— serving each other by helping one another with the problems of life. The law of Christ is to love your neighbor (5:13-14), and this brings the lofty concept of love down to earth. To carry someone's burden is to love with cost—it requires effort, and is not easy. One form of burden bearing is 6:1.

- **v 3-4**

  Be humble, not comparing ourselves with others (i.e. being conceited), but serving them instead. Humility means accepting that we are nothing (v 3): i.e. all that we have is given to us by Christ; it is not our own achievement. Instead of comparing ourselves with others, we should "test [our] own actions" (v 4)—to assess our own gifts and opportunities, and how we are using them. The sign of this is that when surrounded by those less gifted than us, we don't feel superior; and when with those more gifted, we don't feel useless. We are measuring ourselves against ourselves, rather than against others.

- **v 5**

  This looks like a contradiction of verse 2! But "load" is not the same as "burdens". Burdens = heavy weight; load = a backpack. Our load is our own set of liabilities and opportunities, weaknesses and gifts. We don't share or give those to others. We must look at our work today and judge it according to what God has given us, what we are struggling with, and so on.

  NOTE: This makes us slow to judge. If someone snaps at us, we will think, "I don't know what pressures they are facing, nor how much they struggle with self-control. In their situation and with their character, I might have punched instead of snapped—maybe they are actually obeying God better than me today, given their load!"

- **v 6**

  Those being taught in the faith should "share all good things" with their teacher(s). This almost certainly means financial support.

- **OPTIONAL: Why will the attitude of verse 3 prevent someone fulfilling verse 2?**

  If we think highly of ourselves—think we are "something"—then we will be slow to give up what we feel we deserve in order to help others.

5. **Which of these is your church fellowship good at? Which of these could you do better?**

   Do focus on the first part of this question before moving on to the second!

- **How could you, as individuals, make a difference?**

  Aim to come up with specific and realistic answers to this.

6. **What is the principle of verses 7-8?**

   That someone "reaps what he sows" (v 7). Paul is using the agricultural processes of reaping (harvesting) and sowing (planting). His point has two parts:
   - *Whatever* you sow, you will reap. If you sow tomato seeds, you won't harvest corn!
   - Whatever you sow, you *will* reap. Things that are sown produce a harvest—perhaps not for a long time, but the harvest of the seed will come.

   If I sow to please my sinful nature—that is, I do what it wants (5:16)—then I will reap destruction. Just as farming has a process, so does moral choice. If you give in to your sinful nature, you reap spiritual breakdown and destruction. So, if I am consistently dishonest, in time my relationships will disintegrate. If I let myself grow more and more envious, I will lose all contentment and become bitter. Sin promises joy, but the harvest is all destruction.

The right choice is to sow "to please the Spirit"—to obey God to please him (rather than to save ourselves, or to disobey God to seek to please ourselves). Wonderfully, as we freely live for God, we "reap eternal life"—real life, both in terms of its quality and its quantity.

○ **OPTIONAL: How do we see sowing to please the sinful nature and reaping destruction, in the world around us and in our own lives?**

Explore More

○ **Read Luke 6:46-49. What are the similarities between Jesus' and Paul's words?**
Both are talking about what you base your life on—and state that this choice has future consequences. Paul talks about harvesting the consequences of what you've sown; Jesus talks about experiencing the outcome of how you've built. And both are encouragements (to live in a way which leads to blessed life / security on the day of judgment), and challenges (to avoid destruction).

○ **How does Luke 6 help us to understand how we sow to please the Spirit?**
By hearing Jesus' word and putting it into practice.

---

7. **What does Paul encourage in both verse 9 and verse 10?**
"Doing good" (v 9); "let us do good" (v 10).

○ **OPTIONAL: Why is it easy to become "weary in doing good"?**
If we are doing it for the wrong motivations, we will become weary. If we want to feel blessed by doing good, and feel tired instead, we'll get weary of doing good for others. If we are doing good to gain recognition but no one notices, we'll get weary. If we are doing it because we think we have to do so as Christians, then we'll grow resentful and stop doing it (or do it joylessly and minimally). If, on the other hand, we do good to please God and to truly love others, then we won't grow weary of it, however tiring, unnoticed, or difficult burden-bearing becomes.

• **What motivations and priorities does he give for doing this? What does he mean, do you think?**
Motivations:
• "We will reap a harvest" (v 9). We will see fruit and benefits (in our own lives and characters, and in those around us), eventually. But just as a farmer has to wait for harvest, so we must wait for the promised reaping.

- Christians are part of a "family" (v 10). Believers are adopted sons of God (4:5-6)—fellow Christians are brothers and sisters. When we do good in our church fellowship, we are doing and being family.

Priorities:

- We are to do good to all, but especially to other Christians. The Christian life is not primarily about meetings, programs, or even conversions—it is about doing good to the person in front of us, giving them what is best (which may be restoring them, 6:1). Notice that we are to *do* good—Paul is thinking of deeds as well as words.

NOTE: The "family" language is helpful here. Strong biological families tend to love each other more deeply, and look out for each other more quickly, than they do for others—but without ceasing to love and support those outside the family. I am particularly keen to do what is best for my wife and children, but that does not mean I neglect to seek to do good to my neighbor or my coworker. So it is with Christians—we are to do good first of all for our family of believers, but such an attitude and commitment will overflow to our treatment of those who are not Christians, rather than constraining it.

8. Why are they telling the Galatian Christians that they must get circumcised to be saved?

- **v 12**

"To avoid being persecuted." The world appreciates "religion" and "morality" in general; but people find it insulting to be told they are too weak and too sinful to save themselves.

- **v 13**

So that "they may boast about your circumcision in the flesh," i.e. so that they will have influence over others.

- **What does this tell us about what they most want in life? (In other words, what they are trusting and worshiping?)**

They want safety; they want to be accepted; they want to be famous and enjoy high status with others. In other words, their ministry is a form of self-salvation, delivering what they think will make them secure and satisfied in life.

9. How is real Christianity different (v 14-15)?

The heart of your real religion is what you boast in. What, in the end, is the reason why you feel you are in a right relationship with God? Paul says he boasts only in the cross of Christ (v 14). He looks to Christ for who he is, and all he does. Real Christians don't boast in Christ *and* the flesh, i.e. what they do. Religious or moral achievements or failures are of no ultimate significance (v 15). What counts is being a "new creation," given new life through faith in Christ and his death in our place. This is why Paul can say that "the world has been crucified to me" (v 14); the world has nothing to offer that he needs, because he has it all in Christ.

10. **How do verses 14-15 provide a summary of the whole letter?**
    - The cross of Christ is all we need to be justified by God (2:15-16), made sons of God (3:26), to be motivated lovingly to obey by keeping his law (5:13-14).
    - So, knowing Christ is all a Christian needs, both to become a Christian and to live as a Christian (2:14-16).
    - It doesn't matter how good or bad someone's religious performance is (e.g. keeping Jewish rituals such as circumcision). What matters is finding our whole being, our complete identity, in Christ: who he is, and what he has given us (5:4-6; 2:3-5).

11. **What four things does living like this produce (v 16-18)?**
    Peace (with God, others, and ourselves); mercy (from God); having "the marks of Jesus" (i.e. suffering) on our body; grace (i.e. undeserved kindness and blessing).

    - **Why are each of these a consequence of loving and living for Jesus, do you think?**
        - *Peace:* With God, because we are justified by Christ's death in our place, and his gift to us of his perfect obedience (2:15-16); with others, because we are free to love them instead of needing anything from them (5:13-15); with ourselves, because we are not anxious about our own performance, knowing that Christ has done everything needed for us (compare 4:7 with 4:9).
        - *Mercy:* Because God has forgiven us through Christ (3:13).
        - *The marks of Jesus:* Loving and living the gospel of grace makes us unpopular, and leads to persecution from those who want to think that they can save themselves (4:29; 6:12).
        - *Grace:* All of God's blessings are available through Jesus, since faith in him makes us sons of God—heirs to all that is his (4:5, 7).

12. **How would you sum up the letter of Galatians in a sentence?**
    There are many good answers to this! Mine might be: The gospel of grace through faith in Christ alone is not just the ABC of the Christian life, but the A to Z—it is all we ever need.

    - **What encouragement and challenge are you taking away from Paul's letter?**
        You might like to ask people to spend some time thinking about this before writing something down, and then sharing it only if they're happy to.

Optional Extra

Read through the whole of Galatians again. It might be best for you as leader to read it all, allowing the members of your group simply to listen and meditate on the wonderful gospel truths that you've studied during these seven studies on this letter.

Go Deeper with the Expository Guide to

Galatians

by Timothy Keller

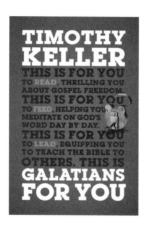

Less academic than a traditional commentary, this expository guide by Timothy Keller takes you through the book of Galatians in detail, exploring how the gospel of grace is not only the ABC of the Christian faith but also the A to Z.

This flexible resource can enrich your personal devotions, help you lead small-group studies, or aid your sermon preparations.

Explore the God's Word For You series

thegoodbook.com/for-you
thegoodbook.co.uk/for-you
thegoodbook.com.au/for-you

Explore the Whole Range

Old Testament, including:

New Testament, including:

  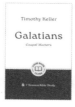 

Topical, including:

Flexible and easy to use, with over 50 titles available,
Good Book Guides are perfect for both groups and individuals.

thegoodbook.com/gbgs
thegoodbook.co.uk/gbgs
thegoodbook.com.au/gbgs

BIBLICAL | RELEVANT | ACCESSIBLE

At The Good Book Company we are dedicated to helping Christians and local churches grow. We believe that God's growth process always starts with hearing clearly what he has said to us through his timeless and flawless word—the Bible.

Ever since we opened our doors in 1991, we have been striving to produce resources that are biblical, relevant, and accessible. By God's grace, we have grown to become an international publisher, encouraging ordinary Christians of every age and stage and every background and denomination to live for Christ day by day and equipping churches to grow in their knowledge of God, their love for one another, and the effectiveness of their outreach.

Call one of our friendly team for a discussion of your needs or visit one of our local websites for more information on the resources and services we provide.

Your friends at The Good Book Company

thegoodbook.com | thegoodbook.co.uk
thegoodbook.com.au | thegoodbook.co.nz
thegoodbook.co.in